The Uniforms of the British Yeomanry

Worcestershire Yeomanry 17

CW01666724

INTRODUCTION: It is generally accepted that research into the uniforms of the Yeomanry Force is complex. For a variety of reasons, certain corps present an even more complicated picture than most of the units and the task of producing a complete and precise record in these instances is particularly difficult. The Worcestershire Yeomanry falls into this category.

The problems in compiling this record are mainly attributable to three factors. Practically no reliable contemporary evidence, pictorial or otherwise, can be traced for the period from formation in 1794 to disbandment in 1827. Numerous changes of headdress and uniform occurred throughout the history of the corps — for example, there were no fewer than five different types of full dress headdress between 1794 and 1890; and certain specific problems relating mainly to details of various items of undress during the period 1850 to 1890 remain unresolved.

Throughout this book, frequent reference has been made to a fine regimental history published anonymously by Q.L. in 1914, entitled *The Yeomanry Cavalry of Worcestershire*. Although this work is one of the best histories produced for a yeomanry regiment, it appears that one or two minor inaccuracies on the subject of uniform have been introduced. These have been noted in the relevant parts of the text.

HISTORICAL NOTES 1794-1827

The Worcestershire Yeomanry trace their origin to the year 1794 when, following a meeting held on 29 April at the Guildhall, Worcester, it was resolved to invite subscriptions in the county towards the defence of the Kingdom, to be devoted to the increase of the military forces of the county. A sum of over £6,000 was subscribed in the county and city, and it was decided to expend this equally between an augmentation of the Militia and the raising of a Corps of Yeomanry Cavalry.

At a further meeting on 15 August it was decided to raise a corps of Yeomanry Cavalry in the county, of which two troops of 36 men each were to be raised at once and £1,000 was voted towards the cost of clothing and equipment. On the 16th, the Committee appointed to manage the subscription issued the following resolution:

'. . . to apply a part of the subscription towards raising and training two Troops of Yeomanry Cavalry. Each Troop to consist of Fifty-six men including officers; for the first of which Troop The Hon. John Somers Cocks has offered his services and has been accepted by the Committee as Captain; Thomas Spooner, Esq., of Leigh, as Lieutenant; George Parker, of the Old House, Gent., as Cornet and Adjutant. Such substantial Householders, or their sons, whether Farmers, Tradesmen, or of any other Occupation, who are willing to enrol their Names in this Corps are requested to sign their names.'

In October 1794 the *Gazette*:

WORCESTER TROOP OF GENTLEMEN AND YEOMEN

To be Captain — The Hon John Summers Cocks (*recte* Somers)

To be Lieutenant — Thomas Spooner, Gent.

To be Cornet — George Parker, Gent.

These commissions bore date 14 September 1794.

On 25 October a parade of the first troop raised was held in the City of Worcester in front of the Unicorn Inn, Captain Cocks being in command. The men were then marched to Powyke Ham for instruction in the rudiments of drill. These drills were continued daily and in two weeks the Troop was reported complete in every particular of equipment as well as in numbers.

On 6 December the first full dress parade of the Troop was held. After the parade, the Troop marched to Madresfield Court, where the men were entertained to dinner by Mr. William Lygon, M.P.

In April 1795, the first Standard was presented to the Troop by the Hon. Mrs. Somers Cocks. The Troop paraded on foot at Worcester Town hall.

A second Standard was presented on 14 June 1797, when the Squadron which was now two Troops, the second having been raised in the autumn of 1796, paraded at Powyke Ham to receive the Guidon for the new troop. This Guidon was styled the county, or Provincial Standard, and had been worked by Mrs. Spooner, who presented it to the Troop commanded by her husband.

A third Troop was raised for the Worcester Yeomanry Cavalry in the course of the summer of 1803, and seven troops of volunteer cavalry. These last were raised at Bromsgrove, King's Norton, Dudley, Wolverley and Kidderminster and two troops at Stourbridge.

In 1811 Colonel Lord Somers[1] resigned the command of the Worcester Yeomanry Cavalry, which he had held since it was raised in 1794. His retirement was greatly regretted by all ranks for the efficiency of the Corps was largely due to the zeal with which he had performed the duties of Commanding Officer during the whole of his service. Lord Somers was succeeded in the command by his eldest surviving son, the Hon. John Somers Cocks in 1813, no Lieut.-Colonel having been appointed in the interval.

With the decisive victory over Napoleon at Waterloo on 18 June 1815 and the peace which followed, the Government adhered to the arrangements that were decided upon in 1802 after the Peace of Amiens. All the Volunteers were immediately disbanded, but no Yeomanry Cavalry were reduced, except by their own consent. Most of the regiments, including the Worcestershire Troops, decided to continue to serve.

New Regulations for the Yeomanry Cavalry were issued by the Government in April 1817.

In the same month, Mr. Addington brought in a Bill to amend the Volunteer Act. The chief points that affected the Yeomanry were that Yeomen should receive billets when called out in aid of the Civil Power; that half-pay officers might hold commissions in the Yeomanry Cavalry without forfeiting their half-pay, and that Yeomen should be exempt from serving as parish officers.

The three Troops assembled for five days' duty at Worcester in May 1817 but there was no inspection.

[1] He had succeeded his father in January 1806 as 2nd Baron Somers, and was himself created Viscount Eastnor and Earl Somers in July 1821.

Inside front cover: *Fig. 3:* Officer, Full Dress, *c.* 1833. From a watercolour by Richard Dighton once owned by L. E. Buckell. (Regimental Collection.)

Front cover: *left:* Kettle Drummer Full Dress 1839; *centre:* Sergeant Full Dress 1831; *right:* Private Full Dress 1860. *At rear:* Farrier Mounted Review Order 1831.

Back cover: *left:* Officer *c.* 1794; *centre:* Captain Mounted Review Order 1897; and *right:* Officer Dismounted Review Order *c.*1905.

In 1818 the annual training of the regiment was held at Worcester in May. In September there was a disturbance in Worcester, known afterwards as the 'Freemen's Riots'. Some building had been erected on the corner of Pitchcroft Ham, known as Little Pitchcroft. This was greatly resented by the populace as being an unwanrrantable infraction of their common rights. On 29 September, a number of the citizens took matters into their own hands and, proceeding to the Ham, commenced to demolish the newly-erected fences and buildings. The Mayor swore in special constables and read the Riot Act, but no one took any notice of him and the constables simply looked on at the process of destruction without interfering. At last a number of the Yeomanry were brought to the scene of action, but being received with a shower of stones, and being glad of any excuse to retreat, they retired to the Star and Garter Yard, and the mob, having completed their work, retired peaceably to their homes.

In June 1819, the annual training was held, as usual, at Worcester. Though the county of Worcestershire still remained free from disturbance, riotous meetings continued to be held in other places, particularly in the manufacturing districts.

Early in December 1827, the Government decided, as part of a programme of economic measures, to disband all the Yeomanry Corps which had not been called out in support of the Civil Power within the last ten years. On receipt of these instructions, Lord Eastnor[2] announced the disbandment of the Corps. All arms and accoutrements were returned to store but members were allowed to retain in their possession their shakos, plumes, jackets, pantaloons and girdles. The Standards were taken under escort to Eastnor Castle, where they were laid up in the Great Hall.

[2]. This was the son and heir of the 1st Earl Somers; he was born in 1788, succeeded as 2nd Earl Somers in 1841, and died in 1852.

Fig. 1: Light Dragoon Helmet or Helmet Cap, 1794-*c.*1823. The cut hackle feather plume thought to be white over scarlet is missing from the left side. This item was replaced by a shako (precise pattern unknown) in 1824. (Regimental Collection.)

Uniform: *1794-1827*

As long ago as 1914 when the history by 'Q.L.' was published, it was made clear that practically no evidence about the uniforms of the first three troops was to be found, and the authors have encountered the same problem. 'Q.L.', states that a pattern of jacket had been received from the Home Secretary according to a minute dated 1796, signed by Lord Coventry and approved by the Committee, but no further detail was given. The only other information offered by 'Q.L.' is as follows: 'There are two other pieces of evidence that are of more importance; one is a miniature of Captain Joseph W. Lavender who commanded the third Troop, which was raised in 1803. This miniature shows a scarlet jacket, laced across the breast with double rows of white lace, with a blue collar. The miniature is now in the possession of Captain Lavender's grandson, Mr. Farull. There was also in existence up to a recent date the actual jacket worn by Lieutenant Thomas Hudson, of Wick House, Pershore. Colonel A. H. Hudson, now of Wick House, states that he remembers seeing the jacket, which cannot now be found, and that it was scarlet and laced across the breast with gold *or* silver cord, and that it had either a blue *or* black collar.'

The whereabouts of this item is now not known. However, there is a very good specimen of the early Light Cavalry or Tarleton helmet worn by the corps *c.*1794-1823 in the Regimental Collection at Worcester (Fig. 1). It has a black skull and a pointed peak, 2½ ins. deep, bound with brass. On the right side of the skull is a brass plate bearing a 'GR' cypher surmounted by a crown and below a scroll inscribed 'Worcestershire'. The crest is of black bearskin and there is a pad at the back edge of the skull with a gold bullion fringe. A turban about 2ins. deep, which is now very worn but obviously of leopardskin, is retained by three double gilt chains each side. Above the peak, each side of the fur crest, is a plate reading 'Yeomanry' – 'Cavalry'. The plume is missing. From the scant information in 'Q.L.' and elsewhere, it would seem that the coloured plate by R. Wymer (Fig. 2) entitled 'A Trooper of the Worcestershire Yeomanry Cavalry dated 1794' is probably a fairly accurate reconstruction. Wymer has introduced a plume of white over scarlet, which may be correct, but the blue or black turban and the silver helmet fittings do not agree with the helmet in the Regimental Collection. The jacket, which is red, has a dark blue collar and cuffs; there are silver horizontal loops and buttons on the collar and cuffs and a white shirt frill appears at the throat. There are about ten loops of white cord or lace set on the garment in pairs on the bias and a row of silver buttons down the front. It is not known what authority Wymer had for this.

The red cloth wings and straps have chainwork and are edged with white; there is also a white fringe to the wings. White or very light buff breeches are worn with black boots. The sword belt and slings are white and surprisingly, there is no pouch belt. The bridle and saddlery are of brown leather and a black fur covers the pistol

Fig. 2: Private, Worcestershire Yeomanry Cavalry, 1794. From a watercolour by R. Wymer in the 'Q.L.' history. Reconstruction of original uniform.

holster; the girth is shown as white. 'Q.L.' noted the early horse kit: 'The saddle was a light one of a hunting pattern, but with a projecting cantle. What little kit there was, was carried in a roll underneath the cantle, to which it was strapped.'

On formation of the corps, the weapons served out to the yeomen were a heavy flintlock pistol and a sword. The exact pattern of sword has not been established, but it was probably either the regular 1780 or 1788 Light Cavalry pattern with a slightly curved blade, a knucklebow guard and a wrought iron (or possibly black leather) scabbard. The pattern for the officers who purchased their own swords would have been basically the same as the yeomen's, but the quality would have been better and there would often have been rich decoration. By about 1800-1810, the 1796 O.Rs' Light Cavalry pattern would probably have replaced the earlier type. This had a much more curved blade, a stirrup guard and either an iron or steel scabbard.

James Willson's chart of 1806 shows the County of Worcester:

Unit	Jacket/ Coat	Facings	Breeches	Lace
Bromsgrove Light Horse	Blue	Yellow	White	Gold
King's Norton Cavalry	Red	Black	White	Gold
Stourbridge 1st & 2nd Troop	Blue	Black collar, blue cuffs	White	Gold

The Dudley Cavalry, Kidderminster Cavalry, Wolverley Cavalry and Worcester Cavalry were not shown.

The late Benson Freeman extracted from the Public Record Office (HO 50/41) notes on the Dudley Loyal Association as follows: 'Blue jacket. Red cloth collar and cuffs. Yellow buttons with the letters 'D.L.C.'. White leather breeches and helmet cap.'

According to 'Q.L.' in 1824 the old leather helmet was replaced by a Light Dragoon shako. Some years ago, details from an example of one of these shakos were noted as rather tall with a lace band round the top, an encrowned boss on the front, chin scales and a shortish upright white over scarlet plume. A yellow sash with two red lines was now worn. There is no information available whether the original red jacket had been modified or replaced by a more modern pattern by 1824, although this would seem very likely. It would also follow that overalls should have replaced the white breeches by this date, although again no evidence has been forthcoming. 'Q.L.' states that a sabretache had been introduced but no confirmation has been found. By 1824, and probably earlier, 12 carbines had been issued per troop, which were attached to a swivel on the pouch belt. This uniform remained in service up to the disbandment of the corps in 1827.

HISTORICAL NOTES 1831-1836

Following outbreaks of organised rioting and civil unrest in the southern counties in 1831, private meetings of Worcestershire magistrates were held and it was decided to reconstitute the disbanded Yeomanry Cavalry so that they would be in readiness to deal with any disturbances which might occur.

The Regiment was officially accepted on 29 April 1831 and, Government sanction having been obtained, Lord Plymouth[1] consented to take command and secured the services of a first class adjutant in Captain W. Emmott, late of the Royal Horse Guards. By the end of March the following year the following nine troops, averaging 50 N.C.O's and men each, had been formed: Worcester; Upton; Stourbridge; Kidderminster; Northfield or King's Norton; Droitwich or Westwood; Tardebigge; Hanbury; Bromsgrove. Another troop was also in process of being raised at Pershore and Evesham. The officers were formally gazetted on 17 June 1831.

As soon as the several troops had been formed and the members enlisted, the somewhat formidable task of clothing and equipping the Regiment was undertaken by Lord Plymouth. For this purpose the Government made an immediate advance of three years' allowance at £3 per head per year for man and horse, amounting to £5,048. The clothing and equipment were obtained in London by the Adjutant and sent to Hewell by canal, whence the various articles were distributed to the captains of troops, who fitted and served out the uniforms on their own troop parades. Five hundred and eighty sets were distributed in the first instance.

In February 1832, one hundred men were raised in Dudley and formed into a squadron. This was styled The Grey Squadron, all the men being mounted on grey horses, and became the 4th, or centre, Squadron of the Regiment. An advance of three years' capitation money was made available for these men also, but the

1. Other Archer Windsor, 6th Earl of Plymouth.

sum granted by the Government was found to be quite inadequate to provide the necessary equipment for the Regiment and Lord Plymouth, with great generosity, made good the deficiency himself by paying over £6,200 into the regimental fund. This large sum appears to have been used for the purchase of the guns, harness, waggons and even the ammunition of the artillery detachment, and for the pay and equipment of the drill sergeants, nothing apparently having been paid by the Government on account of these items.

This same year, the Duchess of Kent and Princess Victoria visited the Earl of Plymouth at Hewell Grange and the whole Regiment turned out to honour the royal party, which was met at Tenbury by the Kidderminster Troop, under the command of Captain Turner, who escorted it to the Hundred Horse, where Lord Foley and the Worcester Troop, under Sir O. Wakeman, were in waiting. After lunch, they left for Worcester, escorted by the Worcester Troop. At Worcester the Troop was relieved by Captain Coventry with the Upton Troop, who escorted the royal carriages to Holt, where the Westwood and Hanbury Troops, under Captain Pakington, took up the duty until Bromsgrove was reached, where Lord Plymouth himself and the Tardebigge Squadron escorted their Royal Highnesses to Hewell, where they were received by the rest of the Regiment and the Artillery detachment with a royal salute.

Lord Plymouth died on 9 July 1833 and was succeeded in the command of the Regiment by his brother-in-law, Major the Hon. Robert Henry Clive, but, as Major Clive was not gazetted until 12 November, the Regiment mustered for Permanent Duty at Worcester on 28 September under the command of Lieut.-Colonel Lord Foley, there being 45 officers and 750 N.C.O's and privates present.

In 1836, the Kidderminster Troop was abolished, most of the members joining the King's Norton Troop, which now became a squadron.

Uniform: *1831-1836*

When the Corps was re-raised in 1831 the uniform adopted was of the popular contemporary Light Dragoon style. A much 'belled' top Light Dragoon shako of the 1830 pattern with a drooping white horsehair plume was worn with a scarlet coatee with light buff facings.

For the period 1830-1840 contemporary pictorial evidence about uniforms is, in general, scanty. However, the Worcestershire Yeomanry is particularly fortunate in that, throughout this period, Richard Dighton, brother of the more celebrated Denis Dighton and himself a talented portrait artist, lived at different dates in both Worcester and Cheltenham. On the reformation of the Corps, Richard Dighton was almost certainly commissioned by the commanding officer, the Earl of Plymouth, to execute portraits of his officers, and it would also appear that further commissions were forthcoming from individual officers and their relatives[1]. The wealth of information contained in these drawings provides a very good, and apparently accurate, picture of the officers' uniform, allowing for minor differences in details such as shako fittings, position of cap lines and sword knots.

The particulars of the *officers' Full Dress* of 1831-1836 are taken mainly from one of the best examples of Dighton's portraits (Fig. 3), now in the Regimental collection but once owned by L. E. Buckell; also the notes made by Buckell on a set of 24 portraits and an important picture of a review (Fig. 4), all of which were seen by Buckell in 1946; and from Reynolds MS in the Victoria and Albert Museum.

Fig. 3 shows the example of Dighton's Worcestershire Yeomanry Officer *c.*1833. This portrait gives a very good idea of the Full Dress uniform prior to *c.*1838. The shako, which is of the 1830 Light Dragoon shape with much belled top, has a black felt body, a black (probably silk) lace band about 1⅜ inches wide round the top and a black patent leather band about 1 inch wide round the base of the cap. The sunken top and peak are in glazed black leather. From the gilt four-leaf holder (some examples are shown as silver) a white horsehair plume rises from the socket and has a gilt retaining ring; the plume drops in front about 11 inches from the point of fall. A circular black silk rosette bearing a gilt crown is located below the plume holder; below the rosette on the front of the cap is a gilt eight-pointed cut star, the centre details of which at this period are uncertain. The silver chin scales are worn, tied up behind the rosette. Double gold cord cap lines circle the shako twice, passing through silver (sometimes shown as gilt) lion's head holders. A black patent leather chin strap secures the cap and the gold lines with gold egg mould ends are looped near to the chains from the white leather pouch belt, which supports a black leather pouch. The picker plate on the belt appears to be hexagonal, with arrow-headed pickers, although oval plates with round bodkin-headed pickers seem to have been more favoured; the silver chains are attached to a circular type silver holder.

The coatee, which appears to be identical to one recorded by L. E. Buckell and P. W. Reynolds, is scarlet, double breasted and has lightish buff collar, cuffs and turnbacks, forming a front base edging about ¾ inch deep at the front and widening round towards the tails. Silver epaulettes can be seen, worn with boxed silver bullions. The three-pointed scarlet pocket flaps on the tails only show two buttons in this drawing whereas it is recorded that the actual garment had three on each flap. The two hip buttons are not visible here. Down the front of the coatee are two

1. L. E. Buckell says 'Most of the portraits show officers, profile, facing to the left of the picture on various coloured horses and drawn to various scales, all have the name of the officer attached.

One or two have horses in more active positions, walking or even trotting. Three officers have black plumes, not white, but the uniform otherwise apparently the same; these are Surgeons or Veterinary Officers. Two or three figures are standing, either by their chargers, or in one case with an orderly (in scale much smaller, holding charger). The orderly has a uniform roughly similar to the officers: white plume, buff facings, white belts, red stripes etc., but he has brass crescents and scales.

All are very carefully painted — thin men, fat men, men with weird noses and weird whiskers.'

rows each of eight buttons which, like the other buttons, are convex ¾ inch silver, bearing 'WYC' in Old English letters, surmounted by a crown. No cuff buttons are shown. The gold lace girdle has two crimson stripes. Very dark grey, almost black, overalls or 'trowsers' with 1¾ inch scarlet cloth stripes are worn with black Wellington boots and spurs. The sword, of 1822 Light Cavalry officers pattern, has a white leather knot with fringe and is carried on black leather slings and a waist belt. A black silk stock and white wrist gloves complete the uniform.

There is a white lambskin saddle rug edged with scarlet cloth, and a brown leather strap. The dark blue shabraque has a broad silver lace edging with a centre leather patch. All the bridle straps, reins, breast plate and crupper are in mid-brown leather. The cross face, head and nose straps are decorated with leather rosettes; there is a long leather fringe from the nose strap or band and from the breast plate. A brass boss can be seen on the bit, breast plate and crupper.

The officer shown in Fig. 3 is very similar to that depicted in Plate 356 in *Military Drawings in the Royal Collection* by A. E. Haswell Miller and N. P. Dawnay. This officer is thought to be Major John Joseph Martin *c.*1833; he clearly has a major's star on his epaulette strap. Also lithographed was the portrait of the Earl of Plymouth *c.*1832 which appears in the Q.L. history. Further information on Richard Dighton's work can be found in an article by W. Y. Carman in Vol. XLV (1967) of the *Journal of the Society for Army Historical Research*.

In addition to the portraits by Dighton, there is a Review picture (Fig. 4) which is dated about 1832. In the foreground are seven mounted farriers in line facing a little to the left of their front; behind them to their right also in line are the artillery with guns.

The officer in the centre is the Commanding Officer, Colonel the Earl of Plymouth. In the background, the Regiment is in line facing front and a troop marches past the Inspecting Officer from the right of the picture. A detailed description follows.

Lord Plymouth: white plume, gilt ring and plume socket, gold cap lines, silver chin scales, black shako, black band at top. Buff collar. Silver epaulettes with button. White pouch belt, plain black pouch. Red jacket, buff turnbacks to skirt. Dark grey trousers with red stripe. White sheepskin edged red. Blue shabraque with silver edge. Bay horse. Gold girdle with two red lines. *The trumpeter* to his right the same, but red plume without retaining ring: red, or mixed buff and red worsted wings, no back piping. No shabraque. Same girdle, belt, pouch and trousers. Dark grey horse. Brass trumpet (something, presumably a bugle, shows on his right hip).

Fig. 4: Review of the Worcestershire Yeomanry, *c.*1832. From a watercolour by Richard Dighton. (Regimental Collection.)

Artillery: gun carriage dark grey; bronze or brass guns (two buckets under left hand near gun). All Artillery wear black shakos (no helmet plate showing), black hair plumes, brass chin scales, black chin strap, plain red collar, red cuff (apparently plain red pointed), two rows of buttons (brass) on front of coat. Red turnbacks to skirts. Dark grey trousers with broad red stripe. Brass shoulder scales and crescents. Two sergeants wear three gold chevrons, much space between. Yellow girdles, two red stripes. Only three horses are shown; very dark brown near horse, the other two dark grey.
Farriers: Black plume, brass chin scales, black chin strap, brass shoulder scales and crescents; buff collar and cuff, but apparently red turnbacks (very vague). Dark overalls with wide red stripe. White sheepskins without edge. White pouch belt over left shoulder, wide black belt over right shoulder. Yellow girdle, (probably two red lines). Dark brown axe pole.

Except for a single farrier, who clearly has the star ornament, none of the artillerymen or farriers shown in the picture have shako plates. This is no doubt an omission by the artist.

It appears that the ORs' *Full Dress* uniform corresponds roughly to that of the officers. The bell-topped shako had a white horsehair drooping plume; no doubt the cap was of lesser quality and had brass and white metal fittings. The red coatee with light buff facings and girdles also agreed in general with those of the officers. Buckell noted that in the only Dighton picture in which a private appeared, the private had a haversack and strap over his shoulder, gilt (brass) shoulder scales, a picker plate on his white pouch belt (but the plate was probably a mistake), black sword belt and slings and grey trousers with red stripes, the grey being of a lighter shade than the officer's.

Almost all Dighton's Worcester Yeomanry portraits show plain collars although seven, of officers, show collars with a fine loop of braid and a button, similar to those of the artillerymen and farriers in the Review picture. (See also cover illustrations of a farrier and a sergeant 1831-3.)

Pistols were served out to the yeomen and there were still twelve men per troop issued with carbines, who now also had bayonets. The swords which were issued were now of the 1821 regular Light Cavalry pattern with three bar guard.

Only one of the Dighton Worcestershire Yeomanry pictures, of an unnamed officer (which appeared at Messrs Parsons, Brompton Road, London, about 1915) depicted *officers in Undress* uniform. Fortunately, it was recorded by P. W. Reynolds and a sketch appears in his MS volumes now at the Victoria and Albert Museum. It was signed Richard Dighton, Cheltenham, and was probably also painted about 1832, as one of the two officers shown is probably Lord Plymouth. Both the officers wore dark blue Undress. The dark blue forage caps had rather large overhanging and stiffened tops with a deepish silver lace band scalloped at both edges, black patent leather plain drooping peaks and narrow black chin-straps. The plain dark blue frock coats were double breasted, with a double row of eight silver buttons in front, silver shoulder scales with crescents and two silver buttons on the round cuffs. A black silk stock shows above the blue stand collar. Front ornaments of silver chains and pickers were worn on the white leather pouch belt and the sword belt and slings were of black leather, worn over the coat. The sword knot was white. Blackish grey overalls or 'trowsers' with broad scarlet stripes, Wellington boots, box spurs and white wrist gloves completed the kit.

Information about the *Undress of the yeomen* during this period is practically non-existent. That there would have been a forage cap, probably of the soft topped muffin variety, goes without saying, but the details are unknown. From regimental accounts of November and December 1831, we learn that blue jackets (which would be drill or stable jackets) served until the arrival of 580 suits of clothing from Messrs. Dolan in December at a cost of £2,260 18s. 5d. and 580 shakos at £333 17s. 9d. These blue drill or stable jackets are noted in the Standing Orders of 1843 and 1854 and probably remained little changed up to about 1860. Although a few changes of uniform had taken place since 1831, the orders would not generally have altered.

HISTORICAL NOTES 1837-1870

Lieut.-Colonel Lord Foley was appointed Lord-Lieutenant of Worcestershire in succession to Lord Lyttelton and retired as Commanding Officer in 1837. On 27 December, Lord Ward was gazetted Lieut.-Colonel. The Hon. R. H. Clive continued as Colonel Commanding. Also in December Her Majesty Queen Victoria was pleased to confer the title of Queen's Own on the Worcester Yeomanry Cavalry in recognition of the Regiment having escorted her when she visited the Earl of Plymouth at Hewell in 1832. The notification of this appeared in the *London Gazette* of 19 December 1837.

A new Troop was raised in 1841 at Witley, the command being given to Captain J. B. Cookes but, according to the inspection parade state, the establishment of privates does not seem to have been increased.

In 1843 the Regiment assembled for Permanent Duty at Worcester on 6 October. Queen Adelaide, who was then at Witley Court, was present at the inspection, having driven over with an escort of Yeomanry under the command of Lieutenant Hemming. During the training, copies of a book containing a short history of the Regiment from 1831 to 1843 were distributed to the Drill Sergeants. This had been compiled by order of Colonel Clive and was printed by Bentley and Co., London, but no author's name is given; it contains little more than extracts from Regimental Orders with the accounts of expenditure and Inspection Parade states from 1831 to 1843, together with an appendix containing the Regimental Rules and Orders.

12 new carbines per troop were issued in 1844, percussion caps being substituted for the old flintlocks.

In 1847 the Regiment assembled at Worcester for eight days' Permanent Duty on 9 September. There were 718 of all ranks present at the inspection. On the 14th, a life-size portrait of Colonel the Hon. R. H. Clive, by Pickersgill (Fig. 7), which had been subscribed for by the Regiment, was presented to him at the Shire Hall.

The Regiment received new clothing in 1848. Carbines were served out to each trooper and the old pistols were returned to store. A further change was made in the arms in 1853, when carbines rifled on the Minie principle were served out in exchange for the old smooth bores and two six-pounder brass guns replaced the original three-pounders. As these required more men to work them, a captain and four drivers were added to the establishment, and 12 of the gunners, who up to this time had been dismounted,

Figs. 5 and 6: Officer's Shako, *c.*1838-1849.

In 1863, on the day before the inspection, Lady Georgina Vernon presented new guidons to the Regiment. The presentation ceremony took place at the Shire Hall and immediately afterwards an engraving of the portrait presented to Captain Emmott in 1855 was given by Lord Dudley to every member of the Regiment who was present.

No provision was made in the Army Estimates of 1864 for the pay of the Yeomanry Cavalry while on Permanent Duty but they were eventually allowed to come out as usual for the annual training and the Regiment assembled at Worcester on 28 July. On the occasion of the review, the ground was kept by a squadron of the Gloucestershire Hussars.

In April 1865, the veteran Adjutant, Captain Emmott, who came of a Lancashire family, died. He was born in 1790 and, having enlisted in the Royal Horse Guards in 1810, served through the Peninsular War, being present at the battles of Vittoria, the Pyrenees, Toulouse and Waterloo. He became Quartermaster of his regiment and eventually retired on half-pay. As has already been noted, he was made Adjutant of the Worcester Yeomanry Cavalry by Lord Plymouth in 1831.

New regulations for the Yeomanry were promulgated in March 1870 and were generally implemented by the annual trainings of the following year.

were now provided with horses. All the artillerymen were found by the Tardebigge Troops. The guns were kept at Hewell and all the gunners came from the Hewell Estate. They had a special sergeant instructor, a pensioner from the Royal Horse Artillery and were drilled and exercised with the guns every Saturday afternoon. The Full Dress of the Artillery detachment was of the same pattern as that of the troopers but blue instead of red. The horses were found by the Colonel.

The Regiment assembled for Permanent Duty at Worcester on 9 September 1854 and was inspected on the 15th by Colonel Griffiths, 10th Hussars. Colonel Lord Ward presented the whole Regiment with new saddlery on his accession to the command.

During the 1855 training, Lord Ward presented a portrait of Captain and Adjutant Emmott to that officer. The picture (Fig. 11), which was painted by Grant, represented Captain Emmott mounted on his favourite charger.

Uniform: *1837-1849*

It will be recalled that the corps was granted the honour of the title 'Queen's Own' in 1837. Several changes in uniform followed, probably appearing from 1838 onwards.

A silver oak leaf lace band was introduced to replace the black top band on the shako. A new plate was also brought in for the front of the headdress; it was still in the form of an

Fig. 7: Colonel the Hon. R. H. Clive, 1847. From a portrait by Pickersgill showing an officer in Review Order *c.*1838-1850, published in the 'Q.L.' history. The horse furniture is basically the same as in Fig. 3, but the rear corners of the shabraque are now rounded and a device has been placed in the corners (see also Fig. 10). There is also a shield-shaped silver plate suspended from the brow band on the animal's forehead.

eight-pointed star but a scroll bearing the title 'Queen's Own' was added above the strap or circlet inscribed 'Worcestershire' over 'Yeomanry Cavalry'; on the convex centre was a foliated entwined single VR cypher. The chin scale bosses now bore the Royal Crest of a lion and crown (Figs. 5 and 6).

The scarlet coatee was retained for all, but the appropriate blue facings on collar and cuffs were adopted. Officers now had a silver check lace edging all round the collar and a silver figuring of tracing braid inside; a row of similar lace edged the pointed cuffs and there was a small figuring on the sleeve above and below the cuff. A silver waterfall was now worn at the waist behind. Several specimens of coatee have only seven buttons per row in front (Figs. 7 and 11). The silver buttons now bore a strap inscribed 'Queen's Own WYC' surmounted by a crown, enclosing a VR cypher. The front edges of the coatee and tails had a turn up or turn back of dark blue. The silver epaulettes were unaltered, as was the crimson and gold girdle. The officers took into service dark blue overalls with broad silver oak leaf stripes for some occasions, but those with the scarlet stripes were retained for certain duties. White trousers were abolished in 1846. About 1840 a silver lace pouch belt, sword belt and slings were introduced for the officers. The lace throughout the belts was of oak leaf pattern on black (or dark blue) Morocco leather. There were silver chains and pickers as front ornaments on the pouch belt. The picker plate was often of oval shape (although hexagonal plates can be seen) and bodkin-headed pickers. The pouches of black leather had silver flaps edged with engraved leaf and bore a gilt VR entwined foliated cypher surmounted by a gilt crown. The belt had a silver buckle, slide and tip. White gauntlet gloves were introduced. These changes can be seen in the portrait of Colonel the Hon. R. H. Clive *c.*1847 by Pickersgill (Fig. 7).

Apart from the new blue facings and a gorget patch in silver check lace which was now worn on the front of the collar, the men's uniform does not appear to have altered very much. White gauntlets were now also worn by the O.Rs and lighter carbines had been introduced in 1835.

No information is available on the *Undress* uniform although it would seem from the Standing Orders of 1843 that no change had taken place for either officers or men. In 1846 black lamb or sheepskins were substituted for white for all ranks.

A watercolour drawing by Henty Martens, undated, about 1846, does not add anything to our knowledge, although the drawing suggests a shako which is not so bell-topped as the 1831 pattern. However, there is no evidence to support the introduction of another pattern of shako between 1846 and 1850.

Extract from Standing Orders, 1843

ORDERS OF DRESS: (from Memoranda Relative to the Worcestershire Yeomanry Cavalry, London, 1843).

No. 1: Morning Dress. Is, for an Officer in Barracks or Quarters, cap, with oilskin cover, blue frock coat, with scales and white trowsers; but at Parades, and appearing in Public, or visiting his Quarters or Stables in Cantonments, the sword and belt to be worn, with short gloves.

For Non-commissioned Officers and Troopers, blue cap, jacket, white trowsers, and boots or shoes, and short gloves.

No. 2: Evening Dress. Is, for an Officer when he dresses for dinner, scarlet coat with epaulettes, gold sash, laced blue trowsers, cap without oilskin. For Non-commissioned Officers and Troopers after mid-day stable hour, in the Morning Dress, see No. 1.

No. 3: Orderly Officer. The Orderly Officer attends *all* mounted parades, Morning and Evening Dress, with sword and belts; but when on other Duties and at Parades, he will appear as other officers do; when he sits down to dinner the sword may be taken off, but so placed that he can put it on immediately should duty require his attendance, but the pouch and belt must be *constantly* worn, as well as the shoulder scales, on this duty.

No. 6: Field Day Order. Is for all, scarlet coat with scales, grey trowsers, chaco, with oilskin and plume, sash, sword and belts, pistols; horses in curb bridle, saddle, holsters, cloaks buckled on before, sheepskins, shabraques, head collars and chains, and with carbines and short gloves.

Figs. 8 and 9: Helmets 1850-1870 — Other Ranks (*left*), and Officers.

No. 7. Drill Order. Is, for an Officer, frock coat with scales, white trowsers, cap with oilskin cover, sword and belts.

For Non-commissioned Officers and Troopers, blue jacket, cap, white trowsers, sword and belts, carbine, pistol, all in short gloves, the horse in curb bridle, saddle, cloak, holsters, but no sheepskin, head collars or shabraques.

No. 8. Review Order. Is, for an Officer, chaco (without cover), plume, scarlet coat, epaulettes, gold sash, laced blue trowsers, sword and belts, gauntlet gloves, boots and spurs, horse as in marching order.

For Non-commissioned Officers and Troopers, coat, grey trowsers, sash, chaco (without cover), plume, sword and belts, carbine and pistol, guantlet gloves; the horse fully accoutred, and with sheepskin, head collar and chain.

No. 9. Marching Order. Is, for an Officer, chaco, with oilskin cover, plume, scarlet coat with scales, gold sash, grey trowsers, sword and belts; scales of chaco buckled under the chin on all parades, the end of the gold line fastened to the button on the left breast; horse full accoutred and with head collar and rein, sheepskin and sharbraque, the ends of which are to be hooked up over the crup in dirty weather; all in gauntlet gloves.

Non-commissioned Officers and Troopers, chaco with cover, plume, scales buckled under chin, coat scales, grey trowsers, sash, sword and belts, gauntlet gloves, haversack over right shoulder, in which are the stable dress, linen, brushes, etc., ...a nosebag- ....fastened to the rear ring on the saddle behind.

No. 18. Observations. Officers to wear spurs and gloves when in regimentals. The shirt collar *never* to appear above the stock. Non-commissioned Officers and Troopers to wear gloves, spurs and straps to trowsers *at all* parades, except the spurs, which will *not* be worn at the foot drill, morning or evening dress, or in watering order; scales to chaco to be down and buckled under the chin at all parades.

Notes

In the above, 'trowsers' refer to overalls and 'laced' means with the overall stripe; 'crup' is a term for crupper.

No. 4 (for Divine Service) was as No. 8, with short gloves, other ranks without carbine or pistol.

No. 5 (Watering Order) was as No. 1, but horses in curb bridles, saddles and holsters, but without cloak, pistol, sheepskin or shabraque, head collar or chain.

No. 10 (In Aid of the Civil Power) was as No. 9, but without shabraque or plume.

No. 12 (Escort Duties) was, to escort a Royal Personage, Review Order. To escort prisoners, No. 6 without shabraque.

Nos. 13 to 15 dealt with dress while on dismounted duty – No. 15 (On Foot with Side-arms to Drill) being officers in the morning dress, sword and belt, other ranks in stable jacket, cap, white trowsers, sword and belt, short gloves.

1850-1870

During the period 1850-1870, the uniform changed surprisingly little. One major change did occur in 1850, when the old Light Dragoon shako was abolished after some twenty years' service. In its place a Heavy Dragoon helmet was introduced. The new helmets (Figs. 8 and 9) were very sturdy and numerous examples have appeared at sales and in private collections in the last seventy or so years. These helmets have been in varying condition and there have been trifling differences in the metal fittings. The descriptions below are taken from three fine specimens in the Regimental collection at Worcester. The O.Rs' pattern is shown in Fig. 8 and that of the officers in Fig. 9. They are practically identical except for the metal mounts. Strangely, at this date, the skull and peaks of the helmet are of boiled black enamelled leather; the comb or crest over the top is silver plated for officers and white metal for O.Rs; both have vertical plain ventilation slits. The peaks, the binding down the back seam and narrow band round the base of the helmet are of silver plate for the officers and white metal for the O.Rs. The backing to the front plates is, again, silver or white metal, with the ornamental front plate gilt for officers and white metal for O.Rs. The plate itself is in the form of the Royal Arms supporters, within which is a circlet or strap bearing the title 'Queen's Own' over 'Regiment'. In the centre is a convex oval plate, silver for officers and white metal for O.Rs, upon which is a gilt or brass single VR cypher entwined. Below the centre device over the peak are two scrolls in the same metal as the front plate, inscribed 'Worcestershire Yeomanry'. At the top of the plate, the whole was surmounted by the Royal crest (lion and crown) for officers and, for O.Rs, a crown. Lions head holders or bosses support the chin chains, all in silver plate or white metal on a crimson velvet backing. White and scarlet horsehair ridge plumes embellish the comb or crest of the headdress and are secured by a metal rosette or crossbar near the front edge. It is interesting that these plumes have frequently been described as white *over* scarlet; they are, in fact, scarlet *inside* white, and fall down the sides of the helmet to a length of about 11 inches. A third helmet at Worcester is basically the same as Fig. 9 (the officers' pattern) but has a black plume and would almost certainly have been for the Artillery section. (See also Figs. 11 and 15.)

From about 1860 onwards the collars of the *Full Dress* scarlet coatees were reduced in depth and rounded in front for the officers. Gold embroidered badges of rank were placed on the officers' collars; the silver check lace edging was retained round the edges and there was a centre figuring.

Fig. 10: Officer's Shabraque Ornament, *c.*1838-1899. Detail of ornament in rear corners.

About 1860, a completely new design of ornamentation over the officers' cuffs was introduced (Figs. 13 and 14). This distinctive rich figuring was as shown in Fig. 13 for field officers and smaller for the rest (Fig. 16). It was to persist for many years, even after the change from coatee to tunic in 1871. All the other items, gold laced girdles, laced belts, pouches and gaunlets remained the same as they were before 1850. The overall effect can be seen in the portrait in oils of Captain William Emmott, Adjutant 1831-1865, painted in 1855 by Grant (Fig. 11).

There were fewer changes for the men; a rare photograph (Fig. 15) shows a private in *Full Dress* *c.* 1857. By about 1865 the blackish grey trousers of the men were exchanged for dark blue ones similar to the officers' Undress; the broad scarlet side stripes were retained. White sword belts and slings were substituted for black; the shoulder scales were now of overlapping white metal plates and crescents bearing 'Q.O.' within. The silver check lace gorget patches and other detail of the men's uniform can be seen in Fig. 15.

The *Undress* uniform is again a grey area. We know from the Standing Orders of 1854 that a scarlet shell jacket was now worn by officers for evening wear (mess dress) and frock coats were still in service. By 1865 the style of forage cap for officers was probably of the French kepi type with a horizontal peak, but it has not been possible to confirm this. An O.R's drill or stable jacket of this period in the Regimental collection is entirely of plain dark blue cloth, except for scarlet plain gorget patches on the collar, nine silver buttons down the front and one on each blue cloth shoulder strap. There are sergeants' silver lace chevrons, which are on scarlet backing, as is the embroidered crown above; this may be a regimental arm badge rather than indicating a sergeant-major. A sergeant's coatee of the artillery section of this period was recorded by P. W. Reynolds. The dark blue garment had a scarlet collar and pointed cuffs; the gorget patches on the collar were in silver check lace and the edging of the cuffs was also in ⅝ inch check lace. There were two silver buttons over the cuffs at the hind seam and two rows, seven in each, of silver half ball buttons on the double-breasted front. The turnbacks of the coat, including the tails, were scarlet, with two silver hip buttons behind and six similar buttons on the short tails, three on each pocket flap. White metal scales with 'Q.O.' inside the crescents embellished the shoulders; there were silver lace sergeant's chevrons with a silver gun above, surmounted by a silver crown, all of which had a scarlet cloth backing.

It is interesting that the helmet and scarlet Full Dress coatee uniform was retained until as late as 1870. A woodcut of 1869 of a mounted guard of honour, although a back view, clearly shows the coatee with scales, girdles, etc., but the plume holder on the helmets suggests the more modern Albert pattern, and is almost certainly a mistake.

Fig. 11: Captain William Emmott, 1855. From a portrait by Grant published in 'Q.L.' history. Officer's mounted Review Order 1850-1870. Apart from the substitution of the helmet for the shako the uniform and horse furniture agree with that in Fig. 7.

There follows some information from *Continuation of Memoranda Relating to the Worcester Yeomanry Cavalry, 1st April 1843 to 31st March 1854* printed by Woodfall and Kinder, Angel Court, Skinner Street, London, in 1854. On page 1 was an appendix giving 'The Regimental Rules and Orders of the Q.O. Regt. of Worcestershire Yeo: Cav: founded by the Earl of Plymouth in 1831'. There were four paragraphs regarding fines, regulations for each troop and four paragraphs regarding attendance. The Rules and Regulations were approved by His Majesty King William IV on 17 June 1831.

REGIMENTAL ORDERS

No. 1
Morning Dress — Is for an officer in Barracks or Quarters. Cap with oilskin cover, blue frock coat, with scales and grey trowsers; but at Parades, and appearing in Public, or visiting his Quarters and Stables in Cantonments, the sword and belt to be worn, with short Gloves. For Non-commissioned Officers and Privates, blue cap, grey trowsers and boots or shoes and short gloves.

No. 2
Evening Dress — Is for an officer when he dresses for dinner: scarlet shell jacket, white waistcoat and satin stock, laced blue trowsers, cap without oilskin. For Non-commissioned Officers and Troopers after mid-day stable hour, in the morning dress (see No. 1).

No. 3
Orderly Officer — The Orderly Officer attends all mounted parades, morning and evening dress, with sword and belts; but when on other duties and at parades, he will appear as other officers do; when he sits down to dinner the sword may be taken off but so placed that he can put it on immediately should duty require his attendance, but the pouch and belt must be constantly worn, as well as the shoulder scales on this duty.

No. 4
Divine Service — Is, unless otherwise ordered, for an officer: helmet, scarlet coat with epaulettes, sword and silver belt, gold knot, laced blue trowsers, gold sash and short gloves, boots and spurs. For Non-commissioned Officers and Privates: helmet, coat and scales, grey trowsers, sash, sword and belt, short gloves, boots and spurs.

No. 5
Watering Order — For Officers, Non-commissioned Officers and Privates in the Morning Dress, see No. 1: horses with curb bridles, saddles and holsters, but without cloak, carbine or sheepskin; no shabraque, head collar or chain and in short gloves.

No. 6
Field Day Order — Is for all, scarlet coat with scales, grey trowsers, helmet, sash, sword and belts; horse in curb bridles, saddle, holsters, cloaks buckled on before, sheepskins, shabraques, head collars and chains, and with carbines and short gloves.

No. 7
Drill Order — Is, for an Officer, frock coat with scales, grey trowsers, cap with oilskin cover, sword and belts. For Non-commissioned Officers and Privates, blue (*sic*) jacket, cap, grey trowsers, sword and belts, carbine; all in short gloves, the horse in curb bridle, saddle cloak, holsters, head collars and chains, but no sheepskin or shabraque.

No. 8
Review Order — Is, for an Officer, helmet, scarlet coat, epaulettes, gold knot and sash, laced blue trowsers, sword and laced belts, gauntlet gloves, boots and spurs, horse as in Marching Order. For Non-commissioned Officers and Privates: coats, grey trowsers, sash, helmet, sword and belts, carbine, gauntlet gloves; the horse full accoutred, and with sheepskin, head collar and chain.

No. 9
Marching Order — Is, for an Officer, helmet, scarlet coat with scales, gold sash, grey trowsers, sword and belts; scales of helmet buckled tight under the chin on all parades; horse full accoutred, and with head collar and rein, sheepskin and shabraque, the ends of which are to be hooked up over the crup in dirty weather: all in gauntlet gloves. Non-commissioned Officers and Privates: helmet, scales buckled tight under the chin, coat scales, grey trowsers, sash, sword and belts, gauntlet gloves, haversack over the right shoulder, in which are the stable dress, linen, brushes, etc. necessary for duty: should it be necessary to carry a feed of corn each man will do so in his nose-bag for that purpose, fastened to the near ring of the saddle behind.

No. 10
In Aid Of The Civil Authorities — This duty will be performed in marching order, but without sheepskins or shabraques.

No. 11 *Inlying Picquets*	Is for all, when on Permanent Duty, the same as field day order, but without sheepskin and shabraque: all in short gloves and to wear the pouch and belt for the day on all duties: if called out, each non-commissioned officer will with his squad proceed to the alarm post or place of parade immediately.
No. 12 *Escort Duties*	To escort a Royal Personage, will be in review order: but to escort prisoners will be in field day order without sheepskin or shabraque, but with head collar and chain.
No. 13 *Under Arms On Foot*	Is for all: helmet, scarlet coat, scales, sash, grey trowsers, sword and belts, boots and spurs, short gloves and with carbines.
No. 14 *On Foot With Side Arms*	Is for all, helmet, coat with scales, sash, grey trowsers, short gloves, boots and spurs, sword and belt.
No. 15 *Ditto to Drill*	Officers in the morning dress, sword and belt. Non-commissioned Officers and Privates: stable jacket, cap, grey trowsers, sword and belt, short gloves.
No. 16 *Guards*	As may be ordered.
No. 17 *Appointments and Accoutrements*	The arms, the bridle and as much of the saddlery as possible to be kept in the men's rooms and ready to be taken up at once, however dark it may be, in the case of necessity.
No. 18 *Observations*	Officers to wear spurs and gloves when in Regimentals. The shirt collar *never* to appear above the stock. Non-commissioned Officers and Privates to wear gloves, spurs and straps to trowsers at *all* parades, except the spurs which will *not* be worn at the foot drill, morning or evening dress, or in watering order: scales of helmets to be down and buckled tight under the chin on all parades. The irons to be kept in oil at all times except when brightened for Parade.

Note that no sabretache is yet listed.

Fig. 12: Colonel William, Earl of Dudley, Officer Commanding 1854-1871. This photograph of Lord Ward in Full Dress about 1855 shows the deeper collar and the crown and star badge of rank on the epaulette strap.

Figs. 13 and 14: Field Officer's Full Dress Coatee, *c.*1860-1870. Note the lower, rounded poste-1855/6 collar, but with badges of rank removed, and the intricate sleeve ornamentation. (Regimental Collection.)

HISTORICAL NOTES 1871-1889

In 1871, the Regiment was re-organised into eight Troops as follows;-

Troop

A Stourbridge	E 1st Upton
B Tardebigge	F 2nd Upton
C Dudley	G Droitwich
D Witley	H Worcester

Captain Hayward of the Tardebigge Squadron retained his commission and continued to share the expenses of the Tardebigge Troop with Sir W. Throckmorton, but commanded the Dudley Troop, which had no Captain, in the field.

The guns were given up and the gun detachment disbanded, although the guns themselves were not returned to Woolwich until 1873. Wesley-Richard carbines were served out to each trooper. This carbine was a small-bore breech-loader with a rifled barrel but was not fired by the old percussion cap. The Wesley-Richard carbines were replaced by the Snider in 1881.

The guidons ceased to be carried in 1872.

In 1874, the Yeomanry Cavalry and the other Auxiliary Forces were placed directly under the orders of the War Office and the Officers commanding the Military Districts, instead of the Lords-Lieutenant of Counties but the latter still made all appointments to first commissions. The new School of Instruction for Auxiliary Cavalry at Aldershot was opened in the spring of this year. All the Drill Instructors were ordered to attend for a course of instruction in March, and all the officers who joined after this date were obliged to go through a month's course also and to obtain a certificate of proficiency before promotion to a higher rank.

On 4 May 1878 Lieutenant-Colonel Lord Sandys retired from the command of the Regiment and Lord Lyttelton was gazetted Lieutenant-Colonel to command in his place; (the latter succeeded as the 8th Viscount Cobham in 1889).

In 1883, for the first year since 1870, the Regiment really began to show signs of improvement in strength. There were also some changes in the organisation, the Witley Troop being disbanded and the King's Norton Troop being raised to replace it. This Troop was made up of the remaining men from the old Witley Troop and a few transferred from the Tardebigge Troop. The new Troop was commanded by Captain the Hon. F. S. A. Hanbury-Tracy and mustered 41 on Permanent Duty. The other Troops were: Stourbridge, Captain J. E. Jameson, 35; Tardebigge, Lieutenent Lord Windsor, 36; Dudley, Captain F. J. Shenstone, 36; 1st Upton, Captain S. G. T. Scobell, 40; 2nd Upton, Captain G. E. Martin, 35; Droitwich, Captain H. F. Vernon, 35; Worcester, Captain J. S. Isaac, 39.

On 5 August 1887, in celebration of the Jubilee of the accession of Queen Victoria, 4,000 local troops paraded on Pitchcroft, Worcester, when the Commander-in-Chief, H.R.H. the Duke of Cambridge, laid the foundation stone of the statue of Her Majesty in front of the Shire Hall. Among the troops present were a troop of the 19th Hussars, the Worcestershire Yeomanry Cavalry, a troop of the Gloucestershire Hussars, the Worcester Artillery Brigade with 10 guns and a squadron of the Staffordshire Yeomanry Cavalry. The Duke, who was staying at Madresfield, was escorted to Worcester by the King's Norton Troop under the command of Captain Hanbury-Tracy. Shortly afterwards, it was announced that Her Majesty had been pleased to alter the title of the Regiment, which was now to be designated the 'Queen's Own Worcestershire Hussars'.

In 1888 some further changes were made in the organisation of the Regiment; the Droitwich Troop was amalgamated with the Worcester Troop, which now became a Squadron, and a new Troop was raised at Malvern, one of the Upton Troops being amalgamated with it. There was a marked increase in the strength of the Regiment this year.

The composition of the Regiment was now as follows:-

Troop

A Stourbridge	E Upton
B Tardebigge	F Malvern
C Dudley	G Worcester (1)
D King's Norton	H Worcester (2)

Fig. 15: Private, Full dress, *c.*1857-1870.

Uniform: *1871-1891*

Lord Sandys assumed command of the corps in 1871. At his direction, the outdated helmets and scarlet coatees were abolished forthwith and a completely new uniform of more modern design was introduced. The headdress was a busby which can only be described as similar in shape to that adopted by the Rifles in 1890, but rather taller. The Q.L. history refers to the busby as being of both lambskin and astrakhan; probably the officers had lambskin and the men astrakhan.

The *officers' Full Dress* was: the lambskin busby which had a scarlet, braided bag (that bore a silver button) on the right side; a silver cord cap line encircled the busby three times; the all-scarlet plume, which was about 8 inches high, of upright horsehair with a vulture feather base and silver retaining ring, was secured in a silver four leaf plume holder. There was no boss in front; the chin chain was silver plated. (Fig. 19). Tailors' notes describe the tunic as 'cut as close fitting patrol lined black silk.' The entirely dark blue superfine cloth garment (Figs. 16-19) had a 2 inches deep collar which was rounded off in front and was fitted with a black tab or stock. The front edges of the skirts were also distinctly cut round. There was a row of ¾ inch silver check lace to the top, front and bottom edges of the collar, which bore gold embroidered badges of rank; there was a small silver button at the top of each narrow, straight silver shoulder cord. Four loops of silver staff cord were at first worn in front, with drops, netted caps and four olivet fasteners; later the loops were changed to ones of silver chain gimp. The edges of the garment were edged all round with ¾ inch silver check lace and the tunic back seams were ornamented as in Fig. 18. A distinctive figuring, which consisted of a chevron of ¾ inch silver check lace to the top of the cuffs, over which was a special figuring in silver tracing braid, was worn on the sleeves. The overall size of the figuring was slightly larger for field officers (Fig. 17).

In 1880-81, the badges of rank were transferred to plaited chain gimp shoulder cords. At some

Fig. 16: Captain William Dowdeswell, *c.*1871. Note the collar lacing and sleeve ornamentation for officers *below* field rank.

stage, probably in the late 1880's, the collar was cut square in front and a plain fine tracing braid with an eye in each corner was introduced inside the collar lace. The netherwear consisted of dark blue overalls with 1¾ inch broad silver oak-leaf lace for full dress and a similar broad scarlet cloth stripe for other purposes, which were worn with Wellington boots and box spurs. From 1886, black knee boots with a 'V' cut in the front of the tops were introduced for mounted duties, together with dark blue riding pantaloons which had either silver lace or scarlet cloth side stripes as on the overalls.

All the earlier pattern silver laced belts, slings and pouch as described under 1837-49 were retained. It was about this date that the officers' sabretache was introduced. The full dress had a black Morocco leather pocket and, at this date, a crimson cloth face (Fig. 19) which was changed to scarlet, probably in 1892. There was a silver oak-leaf lace edging all round the face, both edges of which were scalloped; in the centre was the monogram 'WYC', entwined and foliated, in silver wire; the dark blue velvet scrolls below bore in silver Roman letters 'Queen's Own'; the scrolls were generally edged silver. The whole was surmounted as a rule by a gold embroidered crown (although silver has been noted), with crimson cushions and proper colours, but there are very slightly differing versions. There were three D's at the top for the silver oak-leaf laced slings on black leather. A fine example of a sabretache *c.*1892-1901 from the Regimental collection is shown at Fig. 20.

The swords were no doubt of the officers' Light Cavalry 1822 regulation pattern with a gold knot. White wrist gloves completed the uniform. Leather valises were abolished in 1871.

A portrait of Lord Sandys in full dress about 1878, published as a coloured plate in the Q.L. history, is an overpainted photograph probably prepared specially for the publication in 1913 and mistakenly shows the post 1893 scarlet faced collar.

For the *Other Ranks,* the busby was probably of astrakhan with an all horsehair scarlet plume, white braided bag and white cap lines, but otherwise similar to the officers'. The dimensions of the busby have been noted as: 6 inches deep in front, 8 inches behind and 6 inches across the top from the front to back; the back was shaped to the head like a shako, similar to the 1869 infantry pattern. As far as the authors are aware, no example of the men's tunic of this period has been seen or recorded. Q.L. simply refers to it as 'of blue Hussar pattern with four loops of crimson braid.' No doubt there would have been some form of knot over the cuffs and the back of the otherwise plain all blue tunic would have been ornamented down the seams. Beyond this it would be unwise to speculate. The overalls were of dark blue with ¾inch scarlet cloth stripes down the side seams; Wellington boots and box spurs were worn. From September 1886, blue pantaloons, striped as the overalls, were taken into wear for mounted duties. Black knee boots similar to those of the officers were worn with spurs and foot chains; the Troop officers agreed to pay up to £20 each to meet the cost. When the crimson braided tunic was worn with the scarlet busby bags and stripes on the netherwear, the combination of reds must have been inharmonious. The pouch belt and sword belts and slings were white buff leather and the pouch was of plain black leather. No information is available about the cloaks of either the officers or men, but they were probably plain dark blue. In 1885 the Martini-Henry carbine was taken into service.

The *officers' Undress* headgear was now a dark blue pill box. It had a 1¾ inch deep silver oak leaf pattern lace band and a special top ornament which was made up of a circular cluster of oak leaves and acorns in silver wire embroidery, about three inches in diameter; a narrow black leather chin strap was fitted. For most duties a patrol jacket similar to the Infantry pattern was adopted. It was of blue Venetian cloth, with four loops of black mohair staff cord in front with drops, netted caps and olivets to fasten. The collar, rounded in front, was edged all round with ½ inch black braid and had a figuring inside the edging. All the jacket edges were bordered with 1 inch black mohair which also followed round the back vents. A chevron of 1 inch black mohair edged the cuffs and there was a figuring in fine black tracing braid similar to that on the full dress tunic; there was also figuring below the wide braid on the cuffs. The back seams of the garment each had a double row of black staff cord forming a trefoil in single cord at the top and an Austrian knot at the bottom. There were no shoulder cords or straps.

By about 1888-9 it appears from a photograph that the officers had taken into wear a Heavy Dragoon type frock coat, probably as described under 1892-1900. The photograph is one of only two known to the authors which feature the Undress uniform of the pre-1893 period. These pictures, which can be dated *c.*1886 and *c.*1889, are rather dark and not of good quality. The only surviving examples of uniform which have been located are the officers' pill box, patrol jacket and scarlet mess jacket. As far as the O.Rs are concerned, it is necessary to rely on what little detail can be seen in the two photographs, together with the sketchy information in Q.L. and a few notes by P.W. Reynolds.

From the information available, the *O.Rs' Undress* can be described as: a dark blue pill box

Figs. 17 and 18: Field Officer's Tunic 1871-1902 and 1908 onwards. This example has had the collar squared off and field officer figuring introduced. The rank badges have been transferred to shoulder cords from the collar as authorised in 1880 but the scarlet collar and two extra loops as prescribed in 1892 have not been added.

forage cap with a scarlet band and a button (?piping) and a narrow leather chin strap. Sergeants had silver lace bands and piping in the crown seam, which can be seen in the photographs. The dark blue stable jackets all appear to be plain but any scarlet cord or facings would not show in the photographs. Only the sergeants can be seen to have silver piping all round the collar, silver shoulder cords and silver edging to the cuffs, forming an eye at the top. The N.C.Os' chevrons are silver and at this date all have a crown as an arm badge over the chevrons. Most jackets have ten silver buttons in front, but some have nine and others (sergeants) have only eight. The netherwear was blue overalls with broad scarlet stripes or, from 1886, pantaloons worn with knee boots (which at this date appear to have the tops cut straight) when mounted. White wrist gloves were worn and the pouch belts, sword belts and slings were as described for full dress.

HISTORICAL NOTES 1890-1900

A major change in the organisation of the Yeomanry Cavalry was made in January 1893. The Yeomanry Regiments were paired off in brigades of two regiments, the Worcestershire Regiment being brigaded with the Shropshire and the brigade posted to the 3rd Army Corps. An adjutant was by this arrangement economised and dispensed with in each brigade as one was expected to be able to look after the two regiments. The regiments were organised into squadrons of not more than 100 men or less than 70, all weaker ones being ordered to be broken up, and one Permanent Sergeant only was allowed per sqadron instead of one per troop. The old adjutants were permitted to remain until their five years of service expired. At the same time an effort was made to encourage more attention to musketry practice; a bounty of £1 was offered for every man who passed out of the third-class during 1893 and 1894, and the issue of an additional 20 rounds of ammunition per man was authorised for practice.

A Regimental Order was issued by Lord Cobham giving effect to the Army Order of 22 January 1893, as follows:-

'The Regiment will be reorganised in four squadrons instead of eight and will be as under:-

A Squadron	A and C Troops	Captain the Earl of Dudley
B Squadron	B and D Troops	Captain Everitt
C Squadron	E and F Troops	Major Scobell
D Squadron	G and H Troops	Major Sir H. Vernon

Headquarters and recruiting centres of squadrons:-

SQUADRON	HEADQUARTERS	RECRUITING CENTRES
A	Dudley	Dudley and Kidderminster
B	Bromsgrove	King's Norton and Tardebigge
C	Malvern	Malvern and Upton
D	Worcester	Worcester

The remaining Captains will continue to exercise supervision over that portion of the squadron which is recruited in their own districts, and which at present exists as their troop, and which in future will be termed half-squadron, the present senior troop becoming Right and the junior Left half-squadron.

The Permanent Staff for the future to consist of one Sergeant to act as Regimental Sergeant-Major, and one Permanent Sergeant to each Squadron. The others to remain supernumerary until absorbed.'

The saving effected by this re-organisation amounted to £8,000 annually on the whole of the Yeomanry Cavalry, while the entire strength of the force had by this time dwindled away to a total of 9,530 of all ranks, 300 less than in 1892.

On 9 December 1893 a Regimental Order was issued abolishing the entrance fee of £2 hitherto paid by recruits on joining, but ordering each recruit to pay £1 towards the cost of a pair of knee boots, which became his own property.

During this year, the new Martini-Metford carbines were issued in exchange for the Martini-Henrys.

At the Diamond Jubilee celebration of Queen Victoria in London on 2 June 1897, detachments from 31 of the existing 38 Regiments of Yeomanry Cavalry took part in the procession, the Worcestershire sending one sergeant and 16 rank and file under the command of Major Baldwin. The detachment left by train on the 21st with their horses and were billeted at Paddington for the night.

Fig. 19: Captain in Review Order, *c.*1875. The complete full dress worn 1871-1889 can be seen in this studio portrait. Note the busby, wide silver lace edging to the tunic, sleeve ornamentation and sabretache.

The 1899 annual training took place at Croome Park. On 22 December 1899, in order to meet the demands of the South African War, Lord Windsor issued a Regimental Order asking for volunteers for the Imperial Yeomanry. The headquarters of the Worcester Company of Imperial Yeomanry was established at the Great Brook Street Barracks, Birmingham, where volunteers were directed to present themselves for enlistment by the Assistant Adjutant, Major Baldwin. Mounted drills were carried out at the racecourse at Castle Bromwich and in less then three weeks the Squadron was reported ready for service.

The Worcester Squadron was numbered the 16th Company and posted to the 5th Battalion of Imperial Yeomanry, commanded by Lieutenant-Colonel F. C. Meyrick, late Major, 15th Hussars. The Battalion was composed of the 13th Shropshire Company, the 14th and 15th Northumberland Companies and the 16th, the Worcestershire Company. Although they were not formally gazetted until 13th February, the following officers were appointed to the Squadron:

Captain	A. Bingham Crabbe, late 3rd Hussars
Lieutenant	H. J. Swelwyn, Captain, Q.O. Worcestershire Hussars
	E. A. Knight, Lieutenant, Q.O. Worcestershire Hussars

G. Nettlefold, Lieutenant, Q.O. Worcestershire Hussars

J. T. Lutley, Captain, 5th Batt. Worcestershire Regiment

The government allowed a sum of £25 per head for the clothing and equipment and £40 for each horse, this sum later increased by £5. Lady Dudley presented each yeoman with a badge for the slouch hat; this was a sprig of pear blossom worked in silk (Fig. 25). Lord Windsor provided a set of underclothing for each trooper and a pair of field-glasses for each non-commissioned officer.

The first contingent arrived in South Africa on 3 March 1900 and returned nome on 10 June 1901. A second contingent was sent out early in 1901 and returned home on 8 September 1902, both contingents having served with distinction throughout the campaign.

Uniform: *1891-1900*

Between 1890 and 1893 a number of alterations to the uniform of the Queen's Own Worcestershire Hussars were made following a decision to bring them into line with the uniform of the regular Hussars. As a first step, in 1890 the astrakhan busby of 1871 was abolished and the regulation Hussar busby dating from 1888 was adopted in its place by all ranks (Figs. 23 and 31). The other changes which took place between 1892 and 1893 are described below.

In the *Full Dress*, scarlet collars were introduced to the tunics of all ranks. Although the 1871 pattern officer's tunic (Figs. 16-19) with its distinctive cut, lacing and braiding was retained, two extra loops were added to the front of the garment in order to conform with the six worn in the regular Hussars and some field officers tunics now had a figuring of tracing braid inside the collar lace (Figs. 17 and 18). At the same time the opportunity was taken to modernise the O.Rs.' outdated tunics. The crimson braid was done away with and replaced by white cord ornamentation throughout, in the prescribed regular Hussar fashion. This now included six front loops. The cloth stripes on the overalls of both officers and men were still of scarlet but were changed from single 1¾ inches to double ¾ inch ones. The stripes on the officers' dress overalls remained broad silver oak-leaf lace. Further alterations were that black leather belts were ordered to be discontinued and black leather sabretaches were ordered to be worn on all occasions with the sword, except in review order. Cruppers were abolished throughout the Regiment and regulation jack-spurs with leather straps instead of foot chains were ordered to be issued for the future. Cloaks, capes and jack-spurs from this time forward were obtained from the Royal Clothing Depot, Pimlico, on payment. The officers' mess jacket was also changed from scarlet to blue, and the mess waistcoat from white to scarlet, the lace on both being silver. In Figs. 23, 24 and 31 can be seen the final pattern of Full Dress of the corps, which remained in service for the rest of its existence, apart from the period 1903-1907.

Fig. 20: Officer's Full Dress Sabretache, *c.*1871-1901. This specimen is of the post-1892 period with scarlet cloth face. (Regimental Collection.)

The various orders of dress are shown in the Standing Orders of the Queen's Own Worcestershire Hussars, dated 1892, a summary of which is shown below. These orders would have held good up to 1900, but serge frocks were substituted for stable jackets for the men from about 1896.

For *Officers, Full Dress* consisted of the 1888 regular Hussar pattern busby in black sable or lynx; it had a scarlet cloth bag, which was braided with a silver button; three rows of cap line cord encircled the cap. There was a silver beehive boss in front and the scarlet egret feather plume had a scarlet vulture feather base; the four-leaf plume holder was silver plated, as was the retaining ring and the chin chain mounted on black velvet or leather. Silver double cord cap lines were worn from the busby around the neck, with the egg mould ends looped on the breast near the right shoulder. The dark blue tunics (Figs. 17, 18 and 31) were of the same cut, with lace and braiding, as those described for 1871, but there were some differences. The collars were now faced scarlet and cut square. Examples of some field officers' items show a figuring of tracing braid added around the centre of the collar inside the lace (Figs. 17, 18 and 31). There were now plaited silver chain gimp shoulder cords bearing gold embroidered badges of rank (transferred from the

collar in 1880-81); a small silver button was situated at the top of each shoulder strap. Two additional loops of silver chain gimp increased their number to the regulation Hussar six on the front of the tunics from 1893. The elaborate tracing of eyes down the rows of gimp on the back of the coat were retained but the original staff cord loops were replaced with gimp chain. All the dark blue overalls and riding pantaloons of both officers and men now had side stripes of double ¾ inch scarlet cloth, except for the officers' Full Dress and mess overalls, which retained the single 1¾ inch silver oak-leaf lace. Accoutrements (silver laced belts, slings, pouch and sabretache) were as described in Full Dress for the period 1850-70. Probably about this time the cloth face of the Full Dress sabretache was changed from crimson to scarlet. A plain black leather sabretache was ordered for most purposes except review order from 1892. The officers' swords were still mainly of the 1822 Light Cavalry officer's pattern with a gold knot, but the bowl guard with scroll design may have started to appear by 1893. White wrist gloves completed the uniform of both officers and men.

A small photograph in the authors' collection, of the Regiment marching past at a review in 1897 at Witley, clearly shows that the officer's horse furniture includes a black lambskin with a scarlet vandyked edge and a blue shabraque with rounded front and rear corners, edged round with broad silver lace. The device in the rear corners appears to be that in use as early as 1839-40, which was depicted by Richard Dighton in a print featuring a portrait of Colonel the Hon. Robert Henry Clive in review order about 1839. This was published in an article by W. Y. Carman in the *Journal of the Society for Army Historical Research*, Vol. XLV. The device (Fig. 10) was the monogram QOYC entwined in silver, the garter star below, the whole surmounted by a crown, all in proper colours. Details of the bridle are not clear but a head chain is still in use and the dark crimson throat plume can be seen.

Fig. 21: The Officers in Undress, 1893. (Regimental Collection.)

For all ranks, boots for mounted duties were black knee boots with a 'V' cut in the front of the tops; there is no evidence that officers wore clip-on front bosses; spurs with foot straps were now ordered but some chains persisted. For dismounted duty, Wellington boots and box spurs were worn.

Other ranks also had the regular Hussar 1888 pattern busby, but of O.R.'s quality (Figs. 23 and 24). Otherwise it was as for the officers, but the braid, lines, button and boss were in white. The upright horsehair plume, which was all scarlet, had a white metal retaining ring and was held in a leaf holder of similar metal; the chin chain was of white metal on black leather. The dark blue tunics were of regular Hussar cut, with a scarlet collar and all edging, knots, back braiding and the six loops in front (with caps, drops and figure 8s) in square white Hussar cord. The front of the tunics fastened with six white metal ball buttons.

The tunics of the R.S.M., R.Q.M.S. and most senior sergeants probably had silver cord in lieu of white, although this has not been confirmed. The N.C.O.s' chevrons were of silver lace on a scarlet cloth backing and at least up to about 1897 an embroidered crown appears to have been worn by corporals and above as a regimental arm badge. The white cap lines were as worn by the officers and the netherwear has already been described. For the yeomen, the accoutrements consisted of a white buff leather pouch belt, a plain black leather pouch without ornament and white leather sword belt and slings. By 1898 the sword appears to be of the regular 1885 pattern with a white leather knot.

The Full Dress worn by the men and their horse furniture at this period are well illustrated in the photographs at Figs. 23 and 24.

For *Undress*, *officers* wore the 1871 pattern blue, silver laced pill box forage cap or alternatively a folding fatigue or field service cap (Figs. 21 and 22). The field cap, which was of canoe shape, was all of a dark, dull red (almost crimson) shade of cloth. There were silver braid welts to the top of the cap and on the flaps. A silver embroidered monogram of QOYC entwined was worn on the flap of the cap at the left front. The old infantry-inspired patrol jacket of 1871 was done away with about 1892 and for most duties requiring Undress uniform prior to about 1898 the braided patrol jacket (Fig. 21) was generally worn. It was of dark blue beaver cloth with five loops of 1 inch black mohair braid in front and four rows of black netted olivets thereon; the collar and the front and bottom of the jacket were edged with the same black braid. There was a pointed chevron of black braid on the edges of the cuff, with a figuring of braid on the sleeve above and on the cuff below. The back seams were trimmed with black braid, as were the shoulder straps bearing badges of rank. A figuring of braid appeared round the middle of the collar. According to duties, either pantaloons and knee boots or overalls and Wellingtons were worn. The accoutrements consisted of the Full Dress pouch belt and sword on Full Dress slings; the plain black sabretache was worn throughout. By 1895 a blue serge patrol or fatigue jacket had appeared; it had breast pockets with flaps and buttons, five buttons in front, plain cloth shoulder straps and a stand collar. Later a self belt with a wire buckle was introduced. This garment had replaced the braided patrol jacket for most drill and field work by 1898-9. From about 1890 a dark blue single breasted frock coat (Fig. 21) with a collar edged all round with black 1 inch mohair braid and six loops of similar braid in front was used for off duty wear. The shoulder straps were edged round with black braid and had a black button at the

Fig. 22: Officers in Mess Dress, 1897. Note the dark red folding field caps and heavily laced vests.

Fig. 23: Sergeant Major in Marching Order, 1898. Normally the plume would be removed on the line of march. Note the field service cap strapped over the cloak on the front arch of the saddle. The horse kit still includes the head chain. (*Navy and Army Illustrated*, 1898.)

top. On the cuffs was a plain chevron of black braid with figuring below. Two sets of three black braid streamers with olivets at the top hung down from the waist in the small of the back; there were black silk tassels at the end of each braid streamer. Blue overalls with double scarlet stripes, Wellington boots, spurs and white wrist gloves completed the kit.

The officers' cavalry cloaks were dark blue with turned down collars which were scarlet both sides but otherwise as regulations. They were lined scarlet and had a back strap with two flat buttons and a plated chain and clasp at the throat.

From 1892, as the other uniform changes were taking place, the *men's Undress* items also underwent some alteration. A new pill box forage cap was introduced. It was still of dark blue but there was now a 1¾ inch deep white cloth band and a white welt round the crown seam. The top was decorated with a white centre button and a four part figure radiating outwards with trefoil ends, all in white braid. For N.C.O.s of the rank of sergeant and above the band, piping, button and figure were of silver. A new stable jacket was also taken into wear which was of dark blue with a scarlet collar edged all round with white Hussar cord, white double straight shoulder cords with a small silver button at the top and white cord edging the cuffs, forming an eye over the point. For sergeants and above the cord was silver. The jacket was otherwise quite plain except for 10-12 silver buttons down the front. The N.C.O.s chevrons were of silver padded broken bias lace on a scarlet cloth backing; crowns, when worn, were of embroidered silver and crimson on scarlet, but gold may also have been used. It is not certain whether crowns were still worn by the N.C.O.s' as arm badges but there is a specimen in the Regimental collection which has two silver stripes and a crown. However, by about 1900 this practice appears to have died out, if, indeed, it continued after 1892. L. E. Buckell noted in 1940 that a sergeant's stable jacket as described was said to have been worn for mess up to 1905 with a scarlet vest with a blue collar. The netherwear was as described for mounted or dismounted duties under Full Dress. White wrist gloves completed the kit.

From about 1897 photographs show that the O.R.s had also taken into service a folding field service cap. Unfortunately, the authors have not been able establish its colour positively, but it was almost certainly all red or scarlet. In photographs, the piping to the flap is clearly white and there are two buttons on the front of the flaps. At the same time as the field cap appeared for the men, a blue serge frock was adopted. It fastened down the front with five white metal buttons; there was a button on each breast pocket flap and one at the top of the narrow double white shoulder cords. In 1897 there were wallets on the saddle and head chains were still used. For further details of the various Undress orders, see the extract from Standing Orders 1892 below.

The swords were probably of the regular 1864 pattern by 1893 and of the 1885 type by 1895 and had a leather knot. When mounted, they were carried on the near side of the saddle.

In February 1892, the officer's scarlet mess jacket and white vest, which had been in service from at least 1854 (called a scarlet shell jacket in the Standing Orders of that year) for evening wear, were abolished in favour of a blue jacket and scarlet vest. The jacket was entirely dark blue when adopted, but very quickly, probably from 1893, a scarlet collar was added. A surviving jacket and vest which belonged to Major Sir Henry F. Vernon, Bart., (who resigned on 4 August 1893) are in the Regimental collection at Worcester. He had not troubled to alter the collar to scarlet. The blue stand collar is edged top and front with about ¾ inch silver lace and there is a row of chain gimp round the base. The front and bottom edges of the jacket are edged with silver oak leaf lace; there is similar lace along the edge of the cuffs, rising to a point. Two silver dummies situated either side of the centre peak are at the back of the jacket on the bottom lace edging.

There are silver buttons at the hind seam of the sleeves over the cuffs and a row of tiny seed studs down the left edge of the jacket. Gold embroidered major's crowns are on the outer edges of the plaited chain glimp shoulder straps and there is a small silver button at the top of each strap. The scarlet vest, with a shallow collar, is edged all round with silver ¾ inch oak leaf lace and there is an intricate figuring of plumes, eights and eyes in tracing braid inside the lace and on the pocket slits. The overalls were dark blue with stripes of single 1¾ inch silver oak leaf lace, worn with Wellington boots and dress spurs. A field cap of canoe shape, as described for Undress was worn as required. Allowing for the addition of the scarlet collar, the mess dress described above can be seen in Fig. 22. This pattern of mess dress was to continue after 1902 and in some cases as late as 1911-12.

Queen's Own Worcestershire Hussars Standing Orders 1st May 1892

77. Each recruit on joining will receive a free kit consisting of:–

Forage Cap; Tunic; Jacket; Pair of Overalls; Pair of Pantaloons; Pair of Knee Boots.

These articles of clothing become, when time-expired, the man's own property, but they are not to be used or worn except on duty, or when unifom is authorised to be worn.

The following articles are also to be issued to recruits on joining:–

1 Sword and Belt, complete; 1 Pouch and Belt; 1 Carbine, complete; 1 Pair of Jack Spurs; 1 Pair of Swan-necked Spurs; 1 Busby, complete; 1 Cloak (and Cape); 1 Complete Set of Horse Appointments.

The above articles remain the property of the Commanding Officer.

78. Recruits and Members of the Corps generally, are absolutely forbidden to obtain or use articles of uniform or clothing which are not strictly regimental issue.

DRESS AND EQUIPMENT

106. The following tables contain instructions regarding 'the Orders Parade' in which the Officers, Non-Commissioned Officers and Private Yeomen of the Queen's Own Worcestershire Hussars are to turn out on different occasions, and the mode in which the various articles of equipment are to be carried.

Mounted Duties

i. Review Order; to be worn when the Sovereign, or the Lord Lieutenant of the County is present; for royal escorts and guards of honour, and at all State ceremonies, and otherwise when specially ordered –

Officers	*N.C.O. and men*
Tunics	Tunic
Busbies (plumed) with lines	Busbies (plumed) with lines
Gloves	Gloves
Pantaloons	Pantaloons
Knee Boots and Spurs	Knee Boots and Spurs
Sword and Pouch Belts	Sword and Pouch Belts
Sword and full dress Sabretache	Sword
Horses	*Horses*
Saddlery complete	Saddlery complete
Collar chains	Capes
Capes	Carbines
Holsters	Wallets unpacked
Plumes	
Shabraques	
Lambskins	

ii. Marching Order; to be worn on the line of march, at route marching, in the field, manoeuvres, for inspection by General and Inspecting Officers (unless otherwise ordered), and on other occasions when specially ordered.

Officers	*N.C.O. and men*
Tunics	As for Review Order and in addition Water Bottles and Havresacks
Busbies plumed (except on the line of march and at manoeuvres)	
Gloves	
Pantaloons	
Knee Boots and Spurs	
Sword and Sabretache (plain leather	
Horses	*Horses*
As for Review Order except Sheepskins to be worn instead of Lambskins, and no Shabraque	As for Review Order, with Head Ropes

Fig. 24: Corporal J. Parlour in Review Order, 1896. Compare this off-side view in Review Order with that of the sergeant major in Marching Order in Fig. 23. Note also the crown worn over the chevrons as a regimental arm badge. This practice appears to have been discontinued by about 1900.

iii. Field-day Order; to be used generally for summer Field-days, and when specially ordered.

Officers	*N.C.O. and men*
Same as Marching Order	Same as Review Order
Horses	*Horses*
Same as Marching Order	Same as Review Order

iv. Drill Order; to be used at ordinary drills.

Officers	*N.C.O. and men*
Patrol Jackets	Stable Jackets
Forage Caps	Forage Caps
Gloves	Gloves
Pantaloons	Pantaloons
Knee Boots and Spurs	Knee Boots and Spurs
Sword and Pouch Belts	Sword and Pouch Belts
Sword and plain leather Sabretache	Sword
Horses	*Horses*
Same as Marching Order but without Sheepskins	Same as above

Note: Officers and men are to carry Capes only on the saddle, on all parades.

Dismounted Duties

v. Levee Order; to be worn by Officers only; at Court, Public and Military Balls &c., and when specially ordered

Busbies (with plume and lines)
Tunic
Overalls (silver lace stripes)
Sword and Pouch Belts
Sword and full dress Sabretache
Wellington Boots and Dress Spurs
White Kid Gloves

Note: Officers at a ball removing their swords, take off sword belt and sabretache as well.
Officers attending any entertainment in Levee Order, which necessitates removing their busbies, do not remove the busby lines. The above note applies to Review Order also.

vi. Mess Dress: to be worn by Officers only; at Mess, and when dining during permanent duty with Regiments in the county.

Mess Jacket
Waistcoat
Overalls (silver stripes)
Wellington Boots
Dress Spurs.

vii. Review Order, to be worn at Church Parade, Funerals, Inspection Foot Parades, and when specially ordered.

Officers	*N.C.O. and men*
Tunics	As for Review Order mounted,
Busbies, plumes and lines	except Wellington Boots,
White Kid Gloves	Swan-necked Spurs, and
Overalls (silver stripes)	Overalls are worn instead of
Wellington Boots	Pantaloons, Knee Boots and
Swan-necked Spurs (steel)	Spurs

viii. Drill Order; to be worn when ordered.

Officers	*N.C.O. and men*
Same as Drill Order mounted,	Same as Drill Order mounted,
Except Overalls (red stripes)	with the same exceptions
Wellington Boots and Swan-necked Spurs are worn.	as above.

Note: Pantaloons and Knee Boots are never to be worn on dismounted parades.

General Instructions

107. The pouch belt is the sign of being 'on duty' and is always to be worn by Officers and men on duty, drills and parades.
108. The Orderly Officer wears the pouch belt over the patrol jacket, the pouch belt is never to be worn with the frock coat.
109. The Orderly Troop Sergeant-Majors, Orderly Sergeant and Corporals, and Orderlies generally, appear in drill order if mounted; when dismounted, in stable dress with pouch belts, unless otherwise ordered.
110. The sword belt is worn under the tunic and jacket, and over the frockcoat.
111. The sabretache is to be worn on all occasions when the sword is worn.
112. Officers when in command of, or present with a party under arms, whether for instructional or any other purpose whatever, are invariably to wear swords unless otherwise ordered.
113. The dress of Officers on parade or duty, unless otherwise specially ordered, is to correspond with that of the men.
114. Non-Commissioned Officers on the Permanent Staff are permitted to wear at dismounted Squad and Troop Drills a serge jacket of approved pattern, in lieu of a stable jacket.
115. Non-Commissioned Officers on the Permanent Staff will attend *all drills* of their troops in uniform. This does not apply to Permanent Sergeants giving instruction to individuals who may require it.
116. Officers are not permitted to attend parades in plain clothes at which the men are in uniform.

HISTORICAL NOTES 1901-1914

At the Coronation of King Edward VII on 9 August 1902, the Regiment was repesented by a mounted detachment of one officer and 9 O.Rs which, under the command of Major Baldwin, proceeded by train to London, where it was billetted at Paddington. On the 8th the men paraded at Lord Dudley's house in Carlton Gardens and the detachment had the honour of being inspected by Field Marshal Earl Roberts. On Coronation Day the whole of the Yeomanry detachments paraded in Hyde Park and marched to St. James's, where they were formed up along the Mall.

From December 1904, bayonets were issued and the O.Rs' swords were withdrawn, except for those of the Warrant Officers and Staff Sergeants.

In a Special Army Order dated 21 December 1904 the King had been pleased to approve of the words 'South Africa, 1900-02' being borne on the appointments of the Regiment in recognition of the services of the Worcestershire Company of Imperial Yeomanry during the late war.

On 28 March 1905, Lieutenant-Colonel and Honorary Colonel Viscount Cobham, late Lieutenant-Colonel commanding, was gazetted Honorary Colonel of the Regiment.

The King, in November 1904, had approved the issue of medals to members of the Imperial Yeomanry who had served continuously for a period of ten years without missing a Permanent Duty. These are silver and bear on the obverse the effigy of King Edward VII and on the reverse the inscription 'Imperial Yeomanry, For Long Service and Good Conduct'. The medal is suspended by a yellow ribbon. 33 N.C.Os' and one private (T. Wadams) were found to be qualified for the medals, which were presented by Lord Windsor at Church Parade on 28th May.

The establishment of the new Territorial Force in 1908 brought about many important changes in the organisation of the Yeomanry. The designation 'Imperial' was dispensed with and the establishment of a regiment was fixed at 25 officers (to include an extra Major as second in command and an extra lieutenant to command the machine gun section) and 449 N.C.Os' and privates.

The mounted troops of the several counties were formed into brigades, the Worcestershire Hussars forming the 1st South Midland Mounted Brigade with the Warwickshire and Gloucestershire Regiments.

Fig. 25: The Malvern Detachment 1900 (South African War). The detachment wear the slouch hat with a sprig of pear blossom on the left. Plain khaki serge is worn, with bandoliers, haversacks, water bottles, waist belts and bayonets; cord pantaloons and khaki puttees complete the kit. Lee Enfield rifles are carried along with bayonets.

The scale of pay for privates in the Yeomanry was fixed at 1s. 2d. a day, with an extra messing allowance of 1s. a day, with free rations.

The horses were, if necessary, to be provided by the County Association. A horse allowance of £5 was to be paid to each yeoman who brought his own horse for the whole of the training, a sum of 6s. 8d. being deducted for each day of absence.

An equitation grant of £1 was to be given to each yeoman certified as an efficient horseman.

The annual training to be for 15 days, attendance at eight of these being required for a certificate of efficiency.

The capitation grant was abolished and all equipment and clothing was to be provided by the County Association out of monies supplied by the War Office.

The Yeomanry and the other Territorial Forces were to be subject to military law while embodied.

The term of enlistment to be four years, or as the County Association should decide, but a discharge might be obtained, subject to three months' notice, for £5.

Officers and men of existing corps to be transferred to the new Territorial Force only with their own consent, such consent to be notified before 30 June 1908. No Warrant or Non-Commissioned Officer over 55 or private over 45 years of age to be accepted.

A second Maxim gun was served out to the Regiment in 1910. The machine gun detachment now consisted of one officer, one sergeant, one corporal, 16 privates and two batmen.

The Regiment sent a detachment to London for the Coronation of King George V. The detachment consisted of a non-commissioned officer and five men from each squadron, with a sergeant-trumpeter and a cook, under the command of Major the Hon. C. J. Coventry. It formed part of the 2nd Composite Battalion, Yeomanry Brigade, Commanded by Colonel W. Barrett.

A new riding school at Barbourne was opened in November by the Lord Lieutenant, the Earl of Coventry. The Regiment provided a Field Officer's escort under the command of Major the Hon. C. J. Coventry and a Guard of Honour of five sergeants and 22 rank and file commanded by Major Selwyn.

On 25 November 1913, Lieutenant-Colonel Sir H. F. Grey was gazetted out of the Regiment at the expiration of his term of command and Major the Earl of Dudley was gazetted Lieutenant-Colonel to command in his place.

The Queen's Own Worcestershire Hussars were scheduled to participate in Army Manoeuvres in September 1914 but the outbreak of the First World War in August intervened.

Uniform: *1901-1914*

By a Royal Warrant dated 15 April 1901 and published as Army Order 109, the title 'Imperial Yeomanry' replaced that of 'Yeomanry Cavalry'. This Order also made dramatic changes in the constitution, terms of service, organisation and prescribed training of the Yeomanry Force, which was now to be in the role of mounted infantry.

Among the numerous changes which occurred, rifles, bayonets and saddlery were to be found by the government; a khaki coat, cord pants, gaiters or puttees, hat and spurs were to be provided out

Fig. 26: Badges, Buttons and Shoulder titles 1901-1914. **1** Officer's slouch hat badge 1901-08; gilt with silver pear blossom. Worn by O.R.s but in all gilding metal. On the scrolls, 'Worcestershire Imperial Yeomanry'. **2** O.R.'s shoulder title, 1901-08, gilding metal. **3** O.R.'s field service cap and collar badge 1901-08, gilding metal. Worn by officers in gilt with silver pear blossom. Worded as 1. **4** Button, all ranks, 1901 onwards. Worded as 1, scroll worded as 6. **5** Officer's button, 1905 onwards. Gilt on service dress, silver on blue undress. Round the edge 'Queen's Own Worcestershire Hussars'; on scroll 'South Africa 1900-02'. **6** O.R.'s dress forage cap badge, in white metal. On service dress cap, gilding metal with white metal blossom. On the scrolls, 'Queen's Own Worcestershire Hussars'. **7** O.R.'s shoulder title for service dress 1908-16, gilding metal. (Collection of Lt.-Commander Keith Hook.)

of the contingent allowance. Other alterations to be made in the uniforms and accoutrement are dealt with below.

Much to the regret of all concerned, the distinctive blue, silver- or white-laced Hussar full dress of the Worcestershire Yeomanry was withdrawn from all ranks from 1902, complying with War Office orders — which, incidentally, were not obeyed by all the yeomanry regiments, at least not to the letter, and certainly not, generally speaking, with alacrity. The Worcestershire Hussars, however, acted on the new regulations fairly quickly by introducing khaki uniforms with scarlet facings for both Full Dress (1902-3) and Service Dress (1901-2).

For *Full Dress* purposes and for walking out by the men, the uniform introduced between 1902 and 1903 was of Lancer cut in drab or khaki, with scarlet facings, worn with a felt slouch hat. This particular style of dress was probably inspired by, and adapted from, the uniform of a detachment of Australia's New South Wales Lancers, whose visit to Britain on the occasion of Queen Victoria's Diamond Jubilee celebrations in 1897 had proved so popular. The new khaki Full dress which was adopted by the Queen's Own Worcestershire Hussars was, unlike that of some other yeomanry corps, not intended to be converted for Service Dress purposes as required. A quite separate khaki kit, embellished with scarlet facings, was issued for field service wear. However, as early as 1905, the Full Dress had apparently been found to be both unserviceable and unpopular. This is illustrated in the Regiment's Royal Submission on uniform in 1905, in which the only entry for Full Dress quotes the old blue Hussar uniform for officers and returns a simple nil entry for O.Rs. However, photographs of Church Parade taken at Hewell Camp in 1906 clearly show the whole Regiment still wearing the disliked khaki Lancer kit. By 1908, the unpopular uniform had been abolished and the old distinctive blue Hussar Full Dress had been restored in time for the annual training at Blackmore Park, to the satisfaction of all concerned.

The khaki Lancer Full Dress adopted from 1902-3 consisted of a drab felt slouch hat; the left side of the brim, bearing the regimental badge, was turned up and secured to the body of the hat (Fig. 28). No specimen of this particular hat has been seen by the authors. In spite of one or two sources which describe the pagri or turban worn around the hat as 'all scarlet', a close examination of photographs clearly reveals that only the top five of so narrow folds are dark (scarlet) and there is one broad fold of light drab about 1½-2 inches wide at the base. For the officers, the completely scarlet plume of upright cut hackle feathers was mounted behind either the badge or the turned up

Fig. 27: Officer's Full Dress Tunic *c.*1902-1907. Khaki, scarlet faced Lancer tunic.

left brim of the hat. The O.Rs apparently wore exactly the same pattern of hat, but were distinguished by having a slightly smaller plume (Fig. 28). The cap lines which, for all ranks, were of double drab cord were not attached to the hat, but were worn once round the body and looped with the acorn ends near the top left plastron button in Lancer fashion; the loose or cap ends of the lines passed under the wearer's right arm and were secured round the neck by a runner at the throat (Fig. 28). A good example of this type of officers' tunic can be seen in Fig. 27. The photograph of the tunic reproduced here clearly shows one of a proper Lancer cut, of drab superfine cloth with a scarlet collar, cuffs and piping of a rich drab colour, not the khaki mixture which can be seen in several surviving examples of O.Rs' tunics. There is a row of ¾ inch drab braid to the top and front of the scarlet collar, which bears collar badges in gilt and silver similar to Fig. 26 (3). The scarlet pointed cuffs are edged with ¾ inch drab braid showing a narrow scarlet light on the outer edges; there is similar drab braid edging the three-pointed slash pocket flaps at the back of the tunic on either side of the skirt below the waist. The Lancer pattern plaited drab shoulder cords (normally bearing badges of rank) are mounted on drab. Scarlet Lancer piping is featured in the back seams of the sleeves and body of the garment; there is similar piping down the edge of the centre back vent of the skirts, around the bottom edge and to the front. The buttons, which are all gilt, consist of one small one at the top of each shoulder cord, two similar buttons above each cuff at the hind seam and seven large ones in front, down each side of the plastron, with a flat button at the bottom of each row to go under the girdle. There are two large buttons at the hips behind, with three similar buttons on each of the back skirt flaps.

For *the O.Rs*, the tunic was basically the same as for the officers, except that: the garment was of khaki mixture serge; the double shoulder cords were of straight, narrow drab and the collar only was edged with drab mohair braid; the cuffs were of plain pointed scarlet. Scarlet piping edged the three-pointed flaps on the rear skirts in place of drab braid.

Both the officers and men wore overalls, drab for officers and khaki mixture for O.Rs, with double ¾ inch scarlet cloth side stripes, strapped over black Wellington boots with box spurs.

A Lancer girdle was noted by the authors in 1966 with the tunic shown in Fig. 27. It was of drab with two crimson stripes and was probably the correct pattern for officers. On the other hand, the Q.L. history notes a yellow girdle with two crimson stripes. A girdle to a sergeant's uniform in the Regimental collection at Worcester is definitely yellow with two *scarlet* stripes and was in all probability the type worn by the men.

Tailors' notes describe the officers' pouch belt and pouch worn with this uniform. The belt was of dull tan bridle leather 2½ inches wide, with a gilt buckle tip and slide; there are front ornaments all in gilt, consisting of a whistle and

Fig. 28: Group of O.Rs in Full Dress *c.*1902-1907. O.Rs in the khaki Lancer full dress.

chains with lion's head holder on a circular plate with a decorated edge; the pouch is also of dull bridle leather and has a plain gilt binding to the edge of the flap; the badge, in gilt with a spray of pear blossom in silver, is similar to Fig. 26(3). Sword slings of tan bridle leather carried the sword (probably with a leather knot) from under the tunic. All ranks wore tan leather wrist gloves.

N.C.Os' chevrons were of a drab and white mixture chevron pattern mounted on scarlet cloth and were apparently worn on both arms, at least by sergeants (Fig. 28).

In 1908 the attractive old dark blue Full Dress uniform was restored. It was basically of the pattern already described which was worn up to 1902 but there were some minor changes, mainly to the officers' uniform, which were gradually implemented from 1908 onward. A photograph of a group of officers (Fig. 31), taken at Blackmore Camp in 1908 shows the Full Dress on its reintroduction together with a glimpse of the changes which were eventually to occur. From this photograph it can be seen that the busbies, with egret out of vulture feather plumes, are of the pattern introduced into the regular Hussars from 1888 and in service with this corps from 1890 to 1902. Two of the officers (1st left and 4th from right, standing) have the new ostrich feather plume as per the current Dress Regulations; the all-scarlet colour has been retained. The tunics of the majority of officers are of the old special regimental pattern, which can readily be identified by the rich sleeve ornamentation, the well-rounded fronts to the skirts and especially the flat silver lace which is used round the tunic's edge. No doubt the elaborate braiding of eyes down the back seams of the garment were also present. For more detailed information about his pattern of tunic see the earlier description and Figs. 16-19.

The new style of regulation tunic can be seen on the officer standing 4th from the right in the back row of the group of officers in Fig. 31. The pattern is that prescribed in the 1904 Dress Regulations for all grades of regular Hussar officers. It differs from the regular tunic in that all the lace, braid and chain gimp is silver instead of gold and the dark blue garment has a scarlet collar and follows closely that of the 3rd King's Own Hussars. Undoubtedly, the most noticeable new features are: the simple plain traced single Austrian knots over the cuffs; the collar which is slightly deeper and cut square, with one row only of silver lace at the top and front edges and is traced with a fine plain braid inside the lace; there is a narrow row of chain gimp to the base of the collar (Fig. 37). The ornate braiding of eyes down the gimp on each back seam of the tunic (Fig. 18)

Fig. 29: The Officers in Service Dress, Hewell Camp, 1906. This photograph shows the scarlet embellished khaki service dress of 1902-07.

was removed and made to conform with that of regulation Hussar style. Finally, the fronts of the tunic skirts are cut quite straight and the edging is narrow chain gimp in place of the flat lace. For some unknown reason, two of the officers in Fig. 31, one of whom is the Commanding Officer, Lt.-Colonel Sir H. F. Grey, Bart. (seated front row centre) and an officer standing 1st left in the back row are both wearing the new pattern tunic but their collars and sleeves are braided as for field officer rank in the 1900 Dress Regulations. Photographic evidence suggests that as late as 1913 one or two officers were still in possession of the original style of garment.

There is no change in the way the officers wear the silver cap lines in Fig. 31 and the overalls throughout are the dark blue former undress style with double scarlet cloth side stripes, worn with Wellington boots and box spurs.

As far as the accoutrements in this photograph are concerned, the silver laced pouch belts and sword slings appear to be unchanged, except perhaps that, in those cases where it is possible to distinguish the picker plates clearly, plates of hexagonal shape with arrow headed pickers now seem to be more numerous than the once favoured oval type with the round or bodkin headed pickers. From now on, newly acquired pouches bore gilt ER cyphers with crowns which were worn in company with those of the old encrowned VR pattern; a GR cypher and crown has also been noted. In 1908 the sabretache was not reintroduced; it had been abolished throughout the entire service in 1902. Although many of the officers' swords were still of the Light Cavalry 1822 pattern with three bar guard, several now carry swords with sheet steel bowl guards featuring a pierced scroll design, as adopted by all regular cavalry officers in 1896.

Full Dress was now virtually confined to dismounted occasions such as church parades, attending levees, civic and other ceremonies, also for walking out by the men.

According to the Q.L. history, there were two occasions prior to 1914 when the Q.O.W.H. furnished mounted escorts. These were in 1908 and 1912. Full Dress riding pantaloons were no longer an issue so these items were provided for the men from store. A photograph (Fig. 33) probably taken in 1908 features a subaltern dressed for such duties in the post-1907 period (he also appears to be posing as in a Dighton painting). The tunic is of the regular Hussar pattern which was in the process of being brought in (Figs. 33 and 37). In the horse furniture, it will be seen that no lambskin or shabraque are now used; empty wallets are carried on the front arch and there is a white headrope and a brass bit boss. The throat plume is of dark crimson horsehair and is suspended from a silver ball. As far as is known, there is no evidence that the officers ever took into wear special pantaloons and Hessian boots for levee dress. The uniform used for this purpose in the period 1908-14 was as prescribed in the Regimental Standing Orders 1892 (herein) except, of course that the sabretache was no longer carried.

When the Full Dress reappeared in 1908, the uniform of the ORs was subjected to far less change than that of the officers. One very important alteration which stands out is that the busby was not reissued to the men. In its place a smart staff pattern peaked forage cap, which was all of 'drummers red' with a black patent peak and chin strap and a badge as in Fig. 26(6) was issued; it was of virtually the same pattern as that adopted by the officers for undress about 1905-6. Otherwise the tunics, lines, overalls, Wellington boots and box spurs were as worn up to 1902; no pouch belts, sword belts or slings were now worn except by those warrant officers and staff sergeants still authorised to carry swords. White wrist gloves and, for walking out, whips completed the kit (Figs. 35 and 36).

Probably the last alterations to be made in the Full Dress uniform before the First World War concerned all ranks. By an order of November 1911, the stripes on the overalls of both officers and men were directed to be changed from double scarlet to double ¾ inch white cloth. A memorandum had, in fact, gone out to the regimental tailors, Messrs Hawkes of London, as early as June 1911, requesting that no more items with scarlet stripes should be made up. It further noted that this also applied to the broad silver lace stripes on the mess overalls, which in future were also to be supplied with double stripes of white cloth.

Despite the many uniform changes taking place in 1902 it appears that the old pattern officers mess dress was allowed to continue. This has already been described and consisted of the silver laced dark blue jacket with scarlet collar, a heavily braided and laced scarlet vest and blue overalls with broad silver lace stripes. When required, either the old pill box forage cap or the crimson field service cap sufficed until about 1905-6, when an all red peaked forage cap was introduced (see Undress details).

From about 1909-11, a new pattern mess kit started slowly to appear and in a photograph of C Squadron Ball probably taken at Christmas 1911 (not reproduced) both old and new styles can be seen. The new pattern consisted of a dark blue jacket with no buttons in front, now cut with an open scarlet roll collar, with or without collar badges. There were dark blue cloth shoulder straps bearing silver rank badges and plain pointed scarlet cuffs with no buttons. The low-cut vest was of plain scarlet cloth with four small silver buttons and a white shirt and collar with a black bow tie were worn. For officers wearing the old pattern mess jacket, the overall stripes appear to be broad silver lace and for those with new-style jackets the stripes are of the now

Fig. 30: Private, Mounted Drill Order, 1905. Taken at Eastnor Castle camp in 1905, this photograph shows cap, leather waist belt and bayonet in frog, as introduced in 1904.

obsolete double scarlet cloth described under Full Dress. An interesting feature of the photograph referred to above is that all the O.Rs appearing wear Full Dress tunics, lines, white gloves and overalls bearing the newly authorised white stripes.

From photographs taken during the annual camp at Hewell in 1901, it can be seen that the uniform worn for drill and field wear had taken on a rather patchy appearance, which can be attributed to the issue of the newly authorised khaki Service Dress to some of the men. This khaki uniform was intended to replace the established blue serge Undress.

A photograph of B Squadron (not reproduced) features the members parading in drill order at Hewell. For the most part the men are wearing the items of Undress already described — the folding field service cap with flaps piped white, plain blue serge frock, blue riding pantaloons with double scarlet stripes and black knee boots. In most cases the old white pouch belts are still in service. Among the yeomen are a number of O.Rs who wear the same field service cap, but their frocks are of the newly issued khaki serge pattern. However, the details of this item are not clear. As far as can be seen, the horse furniture includes wallets on the front arch and a white head rope. The carbine is still carried muzzle downwards in the long bucket on the off side of the saddle. Officers who appear in photographs of the 1901 camp also favoured the field service cap, although theirs was of the earlier canoe shape, which had probably been in use since about 1890.

Fig. 31: Lt.-Colonel Sir H. F. Grey, Bart., and the Officers in Full Dress at Blackmore Park Camp, 1908. This shows the Hussar full dress on its reintroduction. The officer standing second from left, back row, wears the red forage cap and blue undress uniform with pouch belt, and is probably the Orderly Officer. The Officer fourth from the left in Lancer full dress is the Adjutant, Captain A. G. McClintock, 5th (Royal Irish) Lancers.

The remainder of the officers' kit consisted of the plain blue serge frock of the pattern taken into wear about 1895-6, although slight alterations appear to have taken place and some frocks now have four patch pockets with flaps and buttons. A blue cloth self belt which fastens with a silver wire buckle in front had been added in some cases. Shoulder chains are not yet in evidence and blue cloth straps suffice. The dark blue riding pantaloons with double scarlet stripes are still in service with black knee boots or, for some, blue puttees and black ankle boots fitted with hunting spurs. Accoutrements were either the old Full Dress pouch belt with the sword on slings or the newly introduced regulation Sam Browne belt which was to replace it for service purposes.

For Madresfield camp in 1902, Regimental Marching Orders for B Squadron dated 28th May direct that O.Rs were to take to camp 'the blue serge, overalls, boots and spurs, forage cap and camp clothes but not the Full Dress. N.B. N.C.Os' and men will parade in hats (slouch), khaki jackets, pants, boots and leggings, cloak rolled to 26 inches as rear pack'. It is interesting that the Undress blue items were still required in 1902, but not the Full Dress tunic. This was probably a stop gap while the new khaki Full Dress was being produced. However, although some items of the old blue Undress were, no doubt, allowed to be worn out by all ranks for perhaps another year, thereafter the old forage caps, officers' blue frock coats, patrol jackets and other blue items became obsolete.

About 1906, in contrast to the prevailing khaki Full and Service Dress, a very smart staff pattern peaked forage cap was authorised for officers. It was all of drummers red with a black patent peak and chin strap; field officers had a silver braided edge to the peak; the badge was similar to Fig. 26 (1). This cap was possibly intended for use with the 1890's pattern mess kit, which had not been withdrawn. By 1908 a companion photograph (not reproduced) to Fig. 31, shows all the officers wearing the new red forage cap. Surprisingly, they are dressed throughout in the 1890's pattern heavily braided frock coat as worn by the Q.O.W.H. until about 1902, many of which had no doubt been taken out of mothballs. The overall are as worn in Fig. 31 for Full Dress, with Wellington boots and box spurs, and the wrist gloves are white. Photographs show these frock coats being worn on special occasions such as Sports Days as late as 1911. Another item reintroduced from 1908 was the officers' blue serge patrol jacket or frock; it was now mainly confined to off duty wear about camp. Basically, the pattern was much the same as that worn in 1901, but by the Elmley Castle camp in 1911 all the officers had replaced the shoulder straps with shoulder chains and collar badges were worn throughout. Some of the frocks had 'self' belts, others did not. Five silver buttons can be seen down the front of the garment, one on each side of the four patch pockets and there are two at each hind seam of the cuffs. For netherwear, either overalls with scarlet stripes (from the next year, white stripes) or plain blue trousers with turn-ups are noted for informal camp wear. White cap covers are fitted to the tops of the red forage caps (see officer 3rd from left, front row in Fig. 34), and tan wrist gloves complete the kit (see officer standing 2nd from left, back row, in Fig. 31.

During the period 1908-14 a dark blue serge frock (Fig. 34) was also brought back into service for the O.Rs. The garment was quite plain, with a blue cloth collar and shoulder straps. There were collar badges, five buttons down the front, one on

Fig. 33: 2nd Lieutenant Williams-Thomas in Mounted Escort Order at Parkfield, Stourbridge, *c.*1908. This photograph was probably taken when Lt. Williams-Thomas performed escort duty in 1908. Note the scarlet stripes on the pantaloons. No shabraque, lambskin or Sabretache. Stripped saddle wallets and white headrope now in use.

each breast pocket flap and one at the top of each shoulder strap. Dark blue plain trousers and black ankle boots or overalls with double scarlet stripes (white after November 1911) were worn with Wellington boots and box spurs. As with the officers, its use was mainly confined to camp off duty wear and social purposes.

According to the Q.L. history, khaki *Service Dress* with scarlet facings was first brought into use by the corps at the annual training at Ross in 1900. It would appear that a minor inaccuracy has crept in here, as the Home Service Yeomanry were not supplied with khaki clothing before 1901, and even then it was for the most part issued gradually from 1901 onwards.

The pattern of Service Dress worn between *c.*1901 and 1907 can be seen in Figs. 29 and 30. The officers' uniform consisted of a staff pattern peaked forage cap (Fig. 29); it was of khaki cashmere cloth, including the peak and had a tan leather chin strap and a scarlet cloth band with a badge in front. The frock or service jacket was in khaki mixture serge with a scarlet stand and fall collar bearing collar badges, although one or two of the officers who appear in Fig. 29 may have had collars of stand-up pattern; all have their khaki cuffs edged with scarlet tubular braid which forms a trefoil over the point. There were scarlet cloth shoulder straps bearing metal badges of rank and a button at the top of each strap. The four pockets were of patch and pleat design with three-pointed flaps, each with a gilt button thereon. Five gilt buttons fastened the garment down the front. Bedford cord riding pantaloons of medium shade, which had scarlet piping in the side seam, were worn either with tan Stohwasser pattern leggings and ankle boots or tan field or knee boots (Fig. 29); hunting spurs with straps were universal. The scarlet piping on the pantaloons was discontinued from 1907. For off duty wear in camp khaki trousers with turn-ups and ankle boots were authorised (Fig. 34). When on duty the Sam Browne belt and tan leather wrist gloves completed the kit. The sword, in a leather covered scabbard, was carried on the saddle when mounted. Although khaki regulation greatcoats of the mounted pattern were introduced from about 1902-3, the old blue cavalry cloaks already described were almost certainly retained until worn out by the older officers.

Fig. 32: The Officers and N.C.Os of B Squadron in Service Dress at Windmill Hill Camp, 1910. Regular pattern S.D. is now worn.

Fig. 34: The Officers in Service Dress. Elmley Castle Camp, 1911. This shows the second pattern of service dress as worn from *c.*1908-12. The officer seated third from left wears the red peaked forage cap and blue undress.

For the other ranks, the headdress was either the felt slouch hat already described under Full Dress, generally with the plume removed for field wear, or a field service cap as in Fig. 30. The cap had a scarlet body and tip, khaki flaps, a turned up front peak and a narrow leather chin strap. There were two small buttons on the front of the flaps; the badge (Fig. 30) was positioned on the body of the cap at the left. The field service cap appears to have been used more often than the slouch hat and, by 1906, the plain khaki regular pattern peaked forage cap had started to replace the folding field service item.

The men's khaki serge frocks were much the same as those worn by the officers (Fig. 32), complete with the same scarlet collar and other embellishments; there were, however, gilding metal shoulder titles (Fig. 26 (2)) which were composed of the letters 'IY' over, on a curve, 'Worcester'. There were gilding metal buttons throughout. Unlike the officers', the lower pockets were not of the patch variety, but were inside pockets with straight cut outside flaps. The Bedford cord riding pantaloons and Stohwasser leggings with ankle boots and spurs were also of the type worn by the officers. The accoutrements consisted of a leather bandolier which, surprisingly, was of a similar pattern as that in service with the regular cavalry from 1903; 50 rounds were carried in five compartments of ten. This regular 1903 pattern bandolier was not served out to the other yeomanry regiments before 1910-11 and was probably purchased out of regimental funds. As early as 1903, photographs of the Tardebigge Troop, Bromsgrove, show waist belts, which may have been of web, in use. However, by 1904 leather waist belts with frogs to carry the bayonets issued in the same year, were in service (Fig. 30). Khaki regulation greatcoats (mounted pattern) with the same shoulder titles as on the service dress frock were issued, probably from about 1903, but a photograph of a dismounted inspection at Blackmore in 1908 shows quite a number of the pre-1901 pattern dark blue cavalry cloaks still being worn by the men.

By 1908 the officers were wearing plain all khaki peaked forage caps and their scarlet embellished Service Dress frocks had been exchanged for the regular pattern plain khaki items. The frocks now had khaki stand and fall

Fig. 35: Group of O.R.s in Full Dress and Undress, *c.*1912-13. Note the drummer's red staff pattern forage cap, the white overall stripes as authorised from November 1911 and the blue serges worn by three of the group.

Fig. 36: Private, Full Dress, 1908-1914. This private wears the full dress of 1908-14 with the white overall stripes of late 1911-14.

Fig. 37: 2nd Lieutenant R. J. Watts in Full Dress, 1913. Lt. Watts wears the full dress tunic which was gradually brought in from 1908. Note the ostrich feather busby plume which replaced the egret feather from 1902.

collars with badges, patch and pleated breast pockets and large plain expanding pockets below the waist, all with a button to the flaps. Drab mixture narrow shoulder cords, each with a button at the top replaced the old straps and there were five buttons down the front of the garment. The buttons throughout were in gilt. Regulation rank braiding in khaki mixture chevron braid was now worn on the cuff, with khaki worsted badges of rank as prescribed. The skirts of the frocks were noticeably longer (Figs. 32 and 34) and the Bedford cord pantaloons, now without piping, appear to be of a slightly darker shade. Sam Browne belts were worn throughout. Photographs taken at Blackmore camp in 1908 show the officers still with crimson throat plumes on their chargers when in field service dress. Another photograph of all the officers in Service Dress at Wind Mill Hill camp in 1910 shows the uniform described above but the buckskin strappings inside the knees of the riding pants appear to be of a distinctly lighter shade, while knee or field boots are universally worn in lieu of leggings. At Bulford in 1913 the uniform is exactly as in 1910 with the exception that all the collars are now cut open in civilian style with turned down collar and turned back lapels; collar badges are now worn above the step of the lapel on the collar. Khaki shirts and ties are practically universal, but three officers have white collars and black ties. The plain khaki peaked forage caps which began to appear for the men from 1906 had completely replaced all other headdresses for service wear by 1908.

From 1907 onwards the O.R's first pattern khaki Service Dress frock with scarlet facings was gradually replaced by the regular cavalry frock or jacket; the scarlet piping was removed from the pantaloons. From 1908 onwards the shoulder titles were exchanged for 'T' over 'Y' over 'Worcestershire' on a curve; at the same time khaki puttees were taken into wear and the leather leggings withdrawn. N.C.Os' chevrons were worn on both arms and were of khaki and white chevron pattern worsted lace. Khaki greatcoats appear to have been in service throughout for the men by 1912. The uniforms worn by the O.Rs up to 1914 can be seen in Fig. 32.

The Regimental Band and Trumpeters *c.* 1838-1914

The first occasion on which the Q.L. history refers to the band, and then only in the briefest possible way, is in 1854. However, the first evidence of the uniform worn by the trumpeters can be found in the watercolour drawing (Fig. 4) to which reference has already been made. A trumpeter in the centre can be seen wearing the red, faced buff, coatee of the O.Rs of the corps. His bell topped shako has the distinctive red plume so often worn by trumpeters and bandsmen. His pouch belt with plain black pouch, yellow and red striped girdle and overalls are all as for the yeomen. He appears to

Fig. 38: Band of the Regiment, 1839. A section of the band, featuring the kettle drummer, from the painting by Pringle.

Fig. 39: The Regimental Band, Hewell Camp, 1906. The band in the khaki Lancer full dress of *c.*1902-7.

be carrying a trumpet but a bugle is slung under his right arm. Apart from the plume, the feature which stands out is his red shoulder wings. The white sheepskin and the remainder of the horse furniture conforms to that of the other O.Rs. The next information appears in 1839, when a painting in oils by W. Pringle entitled 'The Review of the Queen's Own Regiment of Yeomanry Cavalry, Kempsey Hamm' was published as a print engraved by Papprill for Akerman and Co, a section of which appears in (Fig. 38). The picture, which was dedicated to Col. the Hon. R. H. Clive and the officers of the corps, provides vital details of the mounted regimental band of the period. The uniform depicted may well have remained in service up to 1849. Although the original figures are not finely detailed and are only about four to five inches high, it is possible to see that all the band, including the Bandmaster, wear the same uniform. It consists of a tall white fur cap with a small black peak over which is a brass rayed front plate. A drooping scarlet horsehair plume falls from the cap to the height of the top of the front plate. The scarlet coatee with blue collars and blue pointed cuffs appear to be of regimental pattern; there are plain silver gorget patches on the collars. Brass shoulder scales are worn and the cuffs are edged with narrow silver or white piping. There are two rows of seven silver buttons on the front of the coatees and yellow girdles with two scarlet stripes are evident throughout. The dark blue overalls have single scarlet stripes.

The band consists of a Bandmaster and 22 bandsmen, who are made up of a kettle drummer, a side tenor drummer, a cymbalist, 6 cornets, 2 flugelhorns, 3 tenorhorns, 1 baritone, 3 trombones and 4 bombardons. A loose crimson banner which bears the Royal Arms in full colour is visible on one of the kettle drums. Apparently, the side or tenor drum has a large blue panel also bearing the Royal Arms in full colour. Unfortunately, despite exhaustive enquiries, it has not been possible to obtain any information about the band for a period of about 70 years from 1839. No doubt the changes which took place in the rest of the corps were reflected in the band, even if, at times, they were rather behind the rest in receiving new clothing. Surprisingly, the authors have not been able to locate any photographs of the band during the period 1880-1900, normally a prolific period.

A photograph taken at Hewell Camp in 1906 is the next available example of the band's uniform. All the bandsmen wear the officers' pattern khaki Service Dress forage cap with a scarlet band; otherwise the uniform is as worn by the rest of the O.Rs (see post 1900 Full Dress). On either side of the bass drum, which bears the Royal Arms, are, to the left, an officer in Service Dress who is probably the Band President, and to the right, the R.S.M. Standing behind the bass drum is the Bandmaster. It will be noted that this is a brass (or silver) band with no reed instrument (see Fig. 39).

Finally, a photograph taken at the funeral of Viscount Windsor, published in the *Daily Mirror* of 26 February 1909, shows a small section of the band playing. They wear the newly reintroduced blue Hussar uniform with, no doubt, the red staff pattern forage cap, but the bandsmen are distinguished by white bands round the cap.

Guidons of the Worcestershire Yeomanry Cavalry 1831-1872

L.E. Buckell recorded: 'My explanation of these guidons is as follows: On 15 September 1831 the Regiment paraded at Hewell Park to receive guidons from the Countess of Plymouth. "Six cornets came to the front" to receive guidons (the number was not specified), and these would probably have been one each for the five existing double-troop squadrons, and one for the Dudley Squadron expected to be, and actually formed in the following February.

Alternatively, five were squadron guidons and one the Royal, or King's Standard and another made and presented without ceremony to the new Squadron. There would then be one regimental and six squadron guidons, a usual complement.

The Worcestershire Yeomanry Cavalry were not yet, of course, known as the "Queen's Own", which title was bestowed upon them in 1837. The letters "Q.O." were then added to the existing guidons, which accounts for the anomolous "Q.O." coupled with the "W.R.", cyphers.

This set of guidons were laid up in 1863, when new ones were presented, carried until 1872, but these later ones disappeared except for one lodged at Bell Hall, residence of Captain Noel, commanding Stourbridge Troop.'

The seven guidons laid up in 1863 were as follows:

1 and 2 Two were of buff-coloured silk, in the centre a crown between the letters 'Q.O.' and over 'W.R.'

3 One of buff-colour silk, bearing in the centre a crown between the letters 'Q.O.' and over the words 'Worcestershire Yeomanry Cavalry'.

4 One of buff-coloured silk, bearing in the centre a shield of four quarters over the words 'Worcestershire Yeomanry Cavalry' The shield bears in the first quarter a beehive; second, a ship; third, an anchor; four a motto – 'Deo Juvante arte et Industria floret', the words being disposed in a circle.

5 One of crimson silk, bearing a Lion and Unicorn in the centre between the letters 'Q.O.'

6 One of crimson silk, bearing in the centre a Crown over 'W.R. I.V.' between the letters 'Q.O.'

7 One of crimson silk, bearing the Rose, Thistle and Shamrock in the centre between the letters 'Q.O.' In each corner the letters 'W.Y.C.'

The 'Q.O.' (Queen's Own) must have been added to the guidons after the title was conferred by Queen Victoria. This certainly must have been the case with Nos. 1, 2 and 6. No. 7 was probably the first, or King's guidon. 1, 2, 3 and 4 are of the correct colour, buff, the colour the Regimental facings.

Of the guidons carried up to 1872, which disappeared, it is said that the squadrons seem to have had different colours, that of the Hanbury and Droitwich Squadron being green, the Dudley Squadron white and the Stourbridge crimson.